Celestial Dialogues

Frank L. Stapleton

Copyright © 2012 Frank L. Stapleton

All rights reserved. No part of this publication may be reproduced, distributed or transmitted in any form or by any means, including photocopying, recording, or other electronic or mechanical methods, without the prior written permission of the publisher, except in the case of brief quotations embodied in critical reviews and certain other noncommercial uses permitted by copyright law.

Cover Photography—Mark Biehal, westausgang.de

Book Layout & Design—Tracy R. Atkins

Print Edition ISBN: 978-0-692-69219-6 / 0692692193

Contents

PREFACE 1
LIGHT AND DARKNESS CONVERSE 5
SEEING AND HEARING CONVERSE 11
KNOWLEDGE AND OBEDIENCE CONVERSE..........21
PRETENSE AND FRANKNESS CONVERSE...............31
GOOD AND EVIL CONVERSE 43
THE NOW AND THE PAST CONVERSE 55
LIBERALISM AND CONSERVATISM CONVERSE....65
CREATIONISM AND EVOLUTION CONVERSE........79
REVENGE AND FORGIVENESS CONVERSE 91
LIFE AND DEATH CONVERSE 103
FREE SPEECH AND RESTRAINT CONVERSE 115
SPIRITUALITY AND RELIGION CONVERSE..........123

Preface

I have written these sagacious conversations in the hope that they might provide some insight and, perhaps, some clarity in matters that, in one way or another, shape us all. I expect these conversations to clash with the accepted wisdom of our time.

The insight for these conversations came from a vision I had while sitting in a rocking chair in my living room. Let me explain. As I was sitting in the rocking chair relaxing, I fell into a dreamlike state. I don't know whether I was asleep, passed out, or what, but at the same time that I was sitting in the rocking chair, I was also floating above it, looking down at myself. I was shocked at what I saw. For the first time in my life, I saw myself as evil. I had always thought I was a good person, but floating above the rocking chair, I had a different view of myself. I could see my sinful nature and it was ugly. I was horrified. I felt sorry for the person sitting in the rocking chair, as if he were someone else and not me. I gazed at myself for quite some time, thinking how despicable I looked. Then suddenly, the most beautiful beams of light appeared. I felt in my spirit a desire to describe the lights. As I felt this desire, all the words that could possibly be used to describe them were revealed to me. Yet, at the same time I saw all the words that were available to describe the lights; I became troubled in my spirit because I could see that they could not adequately describe their intense luminosity.

When I came to, I felt changed, enlightened. You would have never convinced me, before I had this vision, that I was a sinful person. It made me realize that there is an earthly view and a heavenly view of oneself. It made me question everything. I began to explore Christianity. I read many books on faith and spirituality and scoured the pages of the Bible numerous times. I found the Bible to be a good source to guide my life but at the same time that I believed in it, I had doubts growing inside me with its validity. I was afraid to admit it to myself, but I began to have issues with some of its teachings. The inner turmoil I felt spawned the idea of these conversations. I needed a way to sort out my thoughts and feelings and writing these conversations, debates of sorts, seemed to be the perfect way to do so.

The first conversation I wrote was between Good and Evil. It worked. The dialog I created helped separate my thoughts and gave me clarity on how I felt. I was compelled to write another one. Next, was a conversation between Revenge and Forgiveness where Revenge tells Forgiveness that getting even is a natural response that helps assure survival; therefore, it would be justified. In the conversation between Hearing and Seeing, Seeing tells Hearing that it is better to see than to hear; but Hearing fires back that Seeing will never see that which only Hearing can hear. In a conversation between Pretense and Frankness, Pretense tells Frankness that being pretentious is necessary because you can't truly say what one truly thinks. However, the response of Frankness is a cogent one!

As I wrote these dialogs I didn't take sides. I merely wanted to challenge my belief system and see who would make the best case for their position. My hope is that these conversations will also challenge your belief system and you will find yourself agreeing or disagreeing with a particular point of view. By the time you finish a conversation you will have either changed your view or solidified it. My goal is that these in some way help improve the quality of your life and possibly impact the outcome of your eternal destination.

Light and Darkness Converse

"Show me what you've got," said the Darkness to the Light.

"Let there be light!" said the Light.

"I have already overcome you," said the Darkness.

"I will catch you, for I am fast," said the Light.

"Your source will fizzle out before you catch me," said the Darkness.

"There is enough to overcome you," said the Light.

"Who are you that I should flee from you?" asked the Darkness.

"I am the destroyer of darkness," said the Light.

"Only if your light is eternal," said the Darkness.

"It is," said the Light.

"Then where were you when all things were dark?" asked the Darkness.

"I was behind the darkness where you could not see me," said the Light.

"There is no 'behind me'," said the Darkness.

"You were given a head start," said the Light.

"How did you become light?" asked the Darkness.

"By four words," said the Light.

"What four words?" asked the Darkness.

"Let there be light!" said the Light.

"Why have you invaded my world?" asked the Darkness.

"Because it was good that there be light," said the Light.

"Why is light good and darkness bad?" asked the Darkness.

"Because there can be no life in darkness," said the Light.

"Why must there be life?" asked the Darkness.

"Because in light there is life," said the Light.

"Isn't the fact that I exist prove you shall never overcome me?" asked the Darkness.

"You confuse darkness with death," said the Light.

"But you said that there can be no life in darkness. Is that not death?" asked the Darkness.

"No, it is darkness being exposed to light," said the Light.

"You mean there is no such thing as death?" asked the Darkness.

"There was never a time when a thing did not exist," said the Light.

"Where were 'all things' to be found before there was light?" asked the Darkness.

"In my bosom," said the Light.

"Am I to understand that both darkness and light come from a bosom? What is darkness?" asked the Darkness.

"It is the empty space not yet invaded by the light," said the Light.

"Then the darkness came before the light," said the Darkness.

"Darkness is not a thing. It is a void," said the Light.

"I don't exist?" asked the Darkness.

"A void exists," said the Light.

"When did I become a void?" asked the Darkness.

"You did not become a void. You were always a void," said the Light.

"Was I before you?" asked the Darkness.

"You were my empty pallet," said the Light.

"Is not your pallet limited?" asked the Darkness.

"My pallet has all the colors," said the Light.

"Is not creation flawed?" asked the Darkness.

"Yes it is," said the Light.

"Then thou are not perfect," said the Darkness.

"I am perfect," said the Light.

"How can light create something imperfect?" asked the Darkness.

"I allowed my creation to choose between darkness and light," said the Light.

"Oh! Your creation chose me over you," said the Darkness.

"Some did," said the Light.

"Why did you allow that?" asked the Darkness.

"Because there will be some who will choose the light over darkness," said the Light.

"And what about those who do not choose you?" asked the Darkness.

"They are yours," said the Light.

"Is that fair to them?" asked the Darkness.

"Yes, it is," said the Light.

"You give them free will and, if they don't choose you, you disown them," said the Darkness.

"I am light. There can be no darkness in me," said the Light.

"If your creation doesn't choose you, they automatically become darkness?" asked the Darkness.

"Yes," said the Light.

"Are there enough that choose you to overcome me?" asked the Darkness.

"It is not those that choose me who will overcome you," said the Light.

"Then who will overcome me?" asked the Darkness.

"It is me," said the Light.

"If there is no darkness in you, why do you deal with those that are in darkness?" asked the Darkness.

"Because where there is life, there is still a chance to choose me," said the Light.

"Can you be chosen after death?" asked the Darkness.

"No," said the Light.

"How does one choose you over me?" asked the Darkness.

"They cannot," said the Light.

"How can one choose me over you?" asked the Darkness.

"They are born in darkness," said the Light.

"What do you mean that no one can choose you?" asked the Darkness.

"They don't choose me. They are drawn to me by me," said the Light.

"But at some point they must choose you" said the Darkness.

"I have chosen them," said the Light.

"This is not fair," said the Darkness.

"Who are you to judge me?" asked the Light.

"Even though I am the Darkness, it does not seem fair to me," said the Darkness.

"I knew before creation who would choose me and who would not. It is fair that I draw those that I foreknew who would choose me. Why would I draw those that I know will not choose me?" asked the Light.

"Is this not predestination?" asked the Darkness.

"No, it is taking advantage of knowing something in advance," said the Light.

Seeing and Hearing Converse

"Which is better, to hear or to see?" asked Seeing.

"It is better to hear," said Hearing.

"Hearing is only one thing, while seeing encompasses many things," said Seeing.

"I hear the sounds of many things," said Hearing.

"But you cannot see the colors," said Seeing.

"Did you not know that colors have their own sounds?" asked Hearing.

"I was not aware of that," said Seeing.

"You must close your eyes to see fully," said Hearing.

"I don't understand," said Seeing.

"To really see a thing you must also hear it," said Hearing.

"How so?" asked Seeing.

"When you hear raindrops hit a tin roof, you know more about the raindrops and the tin roof," said Hearing.

"How can hearing raindrops be better than seeing raindrops?" asked Seeing.

"Seeing robs the imagination," said Hearing.

"You don't need an imagination if you can see a thing," said Seeing.

"The imagination is where all creativity is to be found," said Hearing.

"I would not trade seeing for a creative imagination," said Seeing.

"Have you ever closed your eyes for a day?" asked Hearing.

"No," said Seeing.

"Do it, and you will find that all the senses will be magnified," said Hearing.

"So what?" said Seeing.

"Your sense of being returns," said Hearing.

"What good does that do?" asked Seeing.

"It fulfills the purpose for which you were created," said Hearing.

"How so?" asked Seeing.

"Seeing takes too much away from your other senses, and, hence, diminishes your sense of being," said Hearing.

"I've never heard of that before. Do you mean that I am partially responsible for a diminished sense of self-awareness?" asked Seeing.

"Yes," said Hearing.

"What else do you know that I'm unaware of?" asked Seeing.

"You are unaware that, when people speak, they reveal what manner of spirit they are," said Hearing.

"How many spirits are there?" asked Seeing.

"There are approximately 24," said Hearing.

"I don't understand," said Seeing.

"Let me give you an example: When people speak, they reveal by the sound of their voice whether they are haughty, condescending, flippant, arrogant, etcetera," said Hearing.

"Am I to understand that, when people speak, they reveal who they are?" asked Seeing.

"Yes they do, and you cannot know this by way of seeing," said Hearing.

"Why?" asked Seeing.

"Because the eyes see too much," said Hearing.

"How can this be that the eye sees too much?" asked Seeing.

"When it comes to people, the eyes see, but the ears do the discerning," said Hearing.

"Do you mean that when I see someone, I cannot discern who they are?" asked Seeing.

"You can discern their condition, but not who they are," said Hearing.

"How can you know both?" asked Seeing.

"By using your hearing to discern the spirit and your eyes to verify," said Hearing.

"What else do you know that seeing cannot know?" asked Seeing.

"Hearing knows when something is nearby when the eyes can't see it," said Hearing.

"This may be true, but hearing can't even imagine the beauty of a sunset," said Seeing.

"It is also true that words cannot express the beauty of a sunset," said Hearing.

"Then why do you believe that hearing is better than seeing?" asked Seeing.

"Because one is forced to be aware of one's total being when one can't see," said Hearing.

"What is total being?" asked Seeing.

"It is awareness of one's breathing, one's body, one's presence, and one's anatomy," said Hearing.

"Is this not possible with seeing?" asked Seeing.

"It is, but it has to be forced upon a person because one would never think to bring his whole being into seeing," said Hearing.

"Are you saying that people do not totally see?" asked Seeing.

"They see, but they see dimly," said Hearing.

"It seems to me that I see things clearly," said Seeing.

"Can it not be said that you only see things clearly at a certain distance?" asked Hearing.

"Yes," said Seeing.

"Can you see when you sleep?" asked Hearing.

"No," said Seeing.

"Then what is more important when one sleeps; hearing or seeing?" asked Hearing.

"Hearing," said Seeing.

"Can it not be said that hearing is better for the dark and seeing for the day?" asked Hearing.

"I guess it can," said Seeing.

"Can it not also be said that seeing is external and hearing is internal?" asked Hearing.

"I don't understand," said Seeing.

"Hearing invades you while seeing keeps a thing at bay," said Hearing.

"Are you saying that things seen cannot invade you, while a thing heard can?" asked Seeing.

"Yes," said Hearing.

"Do people hear more than they see?" asked Seeing.

"It varies," said Hearing.

"I would much prefer to see a beautiful woman than I would to just hear her," said Seeing.

"You would see her and behold her beauty, but you would not know her until she spoke," said Hearing.

"But it is beauty that most seek," said Seeing.

"Beauty is designed to trap," said Hearing.

"But it is a trap that I want to be caught in," said Seeing.

"Beauty attracts, but hearing holds," said Hearing.

"I can't imagine what it would be like, not to see," said Seeing.

"You can't imagine because you see too much," said Hearing.

"I don't want to imagine," said Seeing.

"Then you will never know all there is to know," said Hearing.

"Give me an example of knowing a thing totally," asked Seeing.

"If you were to see spinach cooking on a stove, you would only know one third of what there is to know about it. But, if you went over to the pot and smelled the spinach, you would know even more. However, it isn't until you actually eat the spinach that will you really know what spinach is. And so it is with seeing; you won't really know it until you've heard it," said Hearing.

"So seeing is incomplete without hearing," said Seeing.

"Yes. It is only a part of the experience," said Hearing.

"I am beginning to see," said Seeing.

"Are you beginning to see the flaw in the question: 'which is better, to see or to hear?'" asked Hearing.

"The question was flawed," said Seeing.

"What have you learned?" asked Hearing.

"To see or not to see depends upon hearing and all the other senses," said Seeing.

"And what does this do for people?" asked Hearing.

"It gives them a total sense of being that cannot be accomplished by seeing alone," said Seeing.

"So, I ask you, which is better, to hear or to see?" asked Hearing.

"Neither," said Seeing.

"Does the universe see?" asked Hearing.

"Yes," said Seeing.

"How?" asked Hearing.

"Through us," said Seeing.

"And what is us?" asked Hearing.

"The whole of us," said Seeing.

"What is the whole of us?" asked Hearing.

"Our sense of hearing, seeing, touching, smelling, and tasting," said Seeing.

"Do you see now that our sense of being was never intended to be linear?" asked Hearing.

"I don't understand," said Seeing.

"It was never intended that we use our senses independent of each other," said Hearing.

"Many there are that do," said Seeing.

"This is true," said Hearing.

"Why do you think this is?" asked Seeing.

"They are fallen," said Hearing.

"Explain," said Seeing.

"In the beginning man walked in the Spirit," said Hearing.

"So?" asked Seeing.

"When one walks in the Spirit, all one's senses are one," said Hearing.

"What other way can one walk?" asked Seeing.

"By sight," said Hearing.

"You're talking about me," said Seeing.

"That's correct," said Hearing.

"Are you saying that seeing is bad?" asked Seeing.

"It is bad when it becomes the only way to experiences the world," said Hearing.

"How can one become whole again?" asked Seeing.

"One's spirit needs to be quickened," said Hearing.

"How can one's spirit be quickened?" asked Seeing.

"From above," said Hearing.

"Above where?" asked Seeing.

"One needs outside help," said Hearing.

"Outside of what?" asked Seeing.

"Outside of seeing," said Hearing.

"What does that mean?" asked Seeing.

"It means that you cannot be quickened by way of sight unless you see a miracle," said Hearing.

"Can one be quickened by way of hearing?" asked Seeing.

"Yes," said Hearing.

"Then hearing is better than seeing," said Seeing.

"Hearing enhances seeing. Hence, those that use their eyes only for seeing will always be looking," said Hearing.

"And what should those who use their whole being to see do?" asked Seeing.

"Look no more," answered Hearing.

Knowledge and Obedience Converse

"Is not knowledge a wonderful thing?" asked Knowledge.

"It is indeed," said Obedience.

"Is not knowledge the most important pursuit of all?" asked Knowledge.

"No, it is not," said Obedience.

"What is more important than the pursuit of knowledge?" asked Knowledge.

"Obedience," said Obedience.

"Obedience?" asked Knowledge.

"Yes," said Obedience.

"Obedience has nothing to do with knowledge," said Knowledge.

"It has everything to do with it," said Obedience.

"How so?" asked Knowledge.

"To pursue knowledge for the sake of knowledge is to deny one's obligation to what is being offered at the present moment," said Obedience.

"I don't understand," said Knowledge.

"To refuse the thing at hand for a thing that one has in mind, is an act of disobedience that will forever cause 'chase after the wind'," said Obedience.

"Surely one has to be knowledgeable about things?" asked Knowledge.

"This is true; but one has to put other things aside to seek it. Hence, it is not worth sacrificing the now moment for a future moment," said Obedience.

"The whole world seeks knowledge. What makes you think your way is right?" asked Knowledge.

"The fact that it is not my way is why. I too sought knowledge, but it wasn't until I embraced what was being offered that the greens became greener and the blues bluer. I now prefer obedience to the pursuit of knowledge," said Obedience.

"I still think that you have to have knowledge to survive in this world," said Knowledge.

"I agree; but to think that knowledge will bring you happiness is a mistake," said Obedience.

"It's a fact, the more knowledge you have, the more successful you'll be," said Knowledge.

"Success is not happiness," said Obedience.

"But it can lead to happiness," said Knowledge.

"It can also lead to destruction," said Obedience.

"What does that mean?" asked Knowledge.

"Knowledge puffs up a person's ego; hence, opening the door for pride to take possession," said Obedience.

"What's wrong with that?" asked Knowledge.

"Pride goes before a fall," said Obedience.

"Tell me then, when is it okay to seek knowledge?" asked Knowledge.

"Knowledge should be sought at the time that it is needed," said Obedience.

"That would stop all progress," said Knowledge.

"It is a mistake to think that the world is progressing," said Obedience.

"Look around you. Can you tell me with a straight face that the world is worse off because of knowledge?" asked Knowledge.

"With the increase of knowledge also comes the decrease of real joy. You look around you!" said Obedience.

"People seem to be happy," said Knowledge.

"They are only happy when they obtain the latest information or the latest new thing," said Obedience.

"Why is this bad?" asked Knowledge.

"Because the thirst for knowledge cannot be quenched," said Obedience.

"What are people to do with their time?" asked Knowledge.

"Love one another," said Obedience.

"Can't they do both at the same time?" asked Knowledge.

"They can," said Obedience.

"Where is the meeting place for the two to be found?" asked Knowledge.

"Where there is a need," said Obedience.

"Are you suggesting that when knowledge is needed it will be supplied?" asked Knowledge.

"Yes," said Obedience.

"I don't believe that," said Knowledge.

"That's because you have an end result in mind," said Obedience.

"This is true. I want to know in advance that the knowledge I might need already exists," said Knowledge.

"Then knowledge is a hedge against the many surprises of life," said Obedience.

"I prefer to think of it as a stabilizing hedge," said Knowledge.

"The cost of stabilizing eventually leads to the total fragmentation of all things," said Obedience.

"I disagree," said Knowledge.

"Knowledge is power. And power corrupts," said Obedience.

"Power in the wrong hands corrupts," said Knowledge.

"Power always ends-up in the wrong hands," said Obedience.

"We have knowledge that can counteract power that falls in the wrong hands," said Knowledge.

"And what about the knowledge that can counteract the knowledge you have to counteract their knowledge?" asked Obedience.

"We will develop new knowledge," said Knowledge.

"So will they," said Obedience.

"It is a game we must play or we'll cease to be," said Knowledge.

"There is a better way," said Obedience.

"And what might that be?" asked Knowledge.

"Seek after the One who is all knowledgeable, and knowledge will be given to you when you need it," said Obedience.

"People have done this and have perished while waiting," said Knowledge.

"Those that were obedient and perished were taken at the right time," said Obedience.

"People want to live as long as they possibly can and it's a known fact that knowledge can increase their lifespan," said Knowledge.

"If you subtract the time spent seeking knowledge, their lifespan has not increased and neither has their joy," said Obedience.

"You talk as if seeking knowledge were not enjoyable and a complete waste of time," said Knowledge.

"It siphons the wonderment and surprise out of life," said Obedience.

"And what does one get for being obedient?" asked Knowledge.

"All that there is," said Obedience.

"And what might that be?" asked Knowledge.

"You would not understand if I told you," said Obedience.

"Try me," said Knowledge.

"You will be at peace and one with the natural order of things. Your hearing will return to you and you will see as you have never seen before. The colors will no longer appear to be flat, but rather appear to be backlit by the sun. Never again will a smile or the brokenhearted go unnoticed. You will be like a light glowing in the dark. Hence, people will seek you out," said Obedience.

"All this I will gain if I drop the pursuit of knowledge?" asked Knowledge.

"Yes." Both are good, but let knowledge be subservient to obedience," said Obedience.

"Then the pursuit of knowledge is not necessarily a bad thing?" asked Knowledge.

"No," said Obedience.

"Why do the masses chase after knowledge?" asked Knowledge.

"Because of its sway," said Obedience.

"What do you mean?" asked Knowledge.

"People who have the knowledge can easily sway those who don't have the knowledge," said Obedience.

"Why would the knowledgeable want to sway the masses?" asked Knowledge.

"For control," said Obedience.

"So, am I to believe that the pursuit of knowledge is really the pursuit of control?" asked Knowledge.

"There are many reasons why people pursue knowledge, but control is the main reason," said Obedience.

"A government requires that everyone obtain a certain amount of knowledge," said Knowledge.

"It does not require a lifelong pursuit of knowledge and neither does God," said Obedience.

"Why do you think that God does not want people to spend their lives seeking after knowledge?" asked Knowledge.

"Because it leaves little or no time for others," said Obedience.

"That does not seem fair to me," said Knowledge.

"It is not fair to you, but it is fair to others," said Obedience.

"Am I not my brother's keeper?" asked Knowledge.

"Yes, you are," said Obedience.

"Then, I disagree." Everyone should be free to choose what he wants to do," said Knowledge.

"And everyone does," said Obedience.

"Were it not for people who broke away from the pack, we would still be stuck in the Stone Age," said Knowledge.

"And what age are you stuck in now?" asked Obedience.

"In an age where knowledge increases daily and people are much better off because of it," said Knowledge.

"I say you're in an age where more than half of the world's population has been left behind," said Obedience.

"So?" asked Knowledge.

"Look what the pursuit of knowledge has done. Have you not noticed the condition of the rivers, the oceans, the landscape, traffic, the number of cars and trucks, airplanes, ocean tankers, the billions of people, not to mention the wars and rumors of wars, land pollution, air pollution, crop pollution, and noise pollution—all because you have interfered with the natural order of things to extend the day, and the lifespan of the human race? If you could, you would do away with the night, and engineer humans to use less air and take up less space. It will come to pass that knowledge will devour all the natural resources, leaving humans no choice, but to kill each other for anything that remains," said Obedience.

"And what is the alternative, to let people die by the millions of natural causes?" asked Knowledge.

"The alternative is to stop before it is too late," said Obedience.

"Too late for what?" asked Knowledge.

"Too late to control the knowledge that's still yet to come," said Obedience.

"What is coming?" asked Knowledge.

"Knowledge that can easily destroy every living thing on earth. It is not knowledge, but the control of that knowledge that will become so burdensome that it will become necessary for governments to lie to their people and eventually take away their freedom to keep them from destroying themselves," said Obedience.

"What's wrong with that?" asked Knowledge.

"Do you trust governments?" asked Obedience.

"No, but what are we to do?" asked Knowledge.

"If you would have asked me 50 years ago or 1,000 years ago, I would have told you to stop the pursuit of any knowledge that has the potential to destroy mankind, but it is too late," said Obedience.

"What does that mean?" asked Knowledge.

"It means that the power to destroy everything on earth is already out of control," said Obedience.

"What do we do now?" asked Knowledge.

"Christians should look up because their redemption draws near. Knowledge seekers should eat, drink, and be merry, for tomorrow they will die," answered Obedience.

Pretense and Frankness Converse

"Why is your nay always nay, and your yea always yea?" asked Pretense.

"Because there is no guile in me," said Frankness.

"What is guile?" asked Pretense.

"Deception," said Frankness.

"Why are you so frank?" asked Pretense.

"Because I loathe pretenders," said Frankness.

"Pretenders hide what they're really thinking for good reasons," said Pretense.

"It is a form of deception, no matter how you look at it," said Frankness.

"If someone asked you what you thought of him, what would you tell him?" asked Pretense.

"I would tell him to be more specific," said Frankness.

"Let's say he wanted to know whether you thought he was smart and attractive. What would you say?" asked Pretense.

"It would depend on why he was asking me," said Frankness.

"I don't understand," said Pretense.

"If I perceived that someone wanted to know in order to improve himself, I would tell him what I thought. If I perceived he just wanted to know what I thought because he was curious, I would not tell him," said Frankness.

"Why not?" asked Pretense.

"Because no good can come from it," said Frankness.

"If it were me and I didn't think he was attractive or smart, I would answer in such a way so as to make him feel good about himself," said Pretense.

"That is because you're a deceiver," said Frankness.

"I don't think of it as deception. I call it caring for someone's feelings," said Pretense.

"You don't care for someone if you're not being honest with him," said Frankness.

"No one likes a blunt person," said Pretense.

"I agree," said Frankness.

"If you agree then why do you continue to be frank?" asked Pretense.

"You confuse bluntness with frankness," said Frankness.

"What's the difference?" asked Pretense.

"There is no discernment or love in bluntness," said Frankness.

"What does that mean?" asked Pretense.

"Discerning the spirit of a person paves the way for frankness, and that is a form of love," said Frankness.

"I still don't understand," said Pretense.

"There are approximately three acceptable motives for asking a question," said Frankness.

"How many unacceptable motives are there?" asked Pretense.

"Roughly seven," said Frankness.

"What are the three acceptable motives for asking a question?" asked Pretense.

"To learn, to change, and to improve," said Frankness.

"What are the seven unacceptable motives for asking a question?" asked Pretense.

"To compare, to trap, to size up, to debate, to test, to use against you, and to discredit you," said Frankness.

"Am I to understand that you'll only answer a question when it's asked for the right reason?" asked Pretense.

"Yes. Frankness is appreciated by those who seek it for the right reason," said Frankness.

"Why have you chosen this way to answer questions?" asked Pretense.

"It is the most efficient use of time," said Frankness.

"How so?" asked Pretense.

"Pretentious people avoid frankness, but sincere people will seek it out," said Frankness.

"I still don't understand why this would be the most efficient use of your time," said Pretense.

"By frankness being targeted at those who really need and appreciate it, there would be no time wasted on those who asked questions for the wrong reason," said Frankness.

"It seems to me that those who asked questions for the wrong reasons are the ones that need it the most," said Pretense.

"It might seem that way, but the fact that they ask questions for the wrong reasons is proof that they don't really want to know," said Frankness.

"That being the case, what do you do when a person asks a question for the wrong reason?" asked Pretense.

"I discern the spirit of his question, and if I determine that he is trying to trap me, I trap him instead with a question," said Frankness.

"Give me an example," said Pretense.

"Let us say that I am a politician and a news reporter asked me whether I thought the government should make the rich pay more taxes. Discerning that this is a trap question, I would respond by asking the reporter whether the government is treating its citizens as foreigners in their own land by making them pay taxes," said Frankness.

"I'm confused. I don't understand," said Pretense.

"When someone asks a question to trap you, he is planning to use your answer against you. Therefore, you ask him a question in such a way that his answer can be used against him," said Frankness.

"This is why I prefer pretense," said Pretense.

"Most do because it takes wisdom to be frank," said Frankness.

"Why do you think most people prefer pretending?" asked Pretense.

"Non-commitment," said Frankness.

"Non-commitment to what?" asked Pretense.

"Non-commitment to others and to the truth," said Frankness.

"Give me proof," said Pretense.

"Has not everything become tentative and abstract?" asked Frankness.

"That's because people don't want to be boxed in with truth," said Pretense.

"Then they will suffer the consequences," said Frankness.

"And what might they be?" asked Pretense.

"For one, the consequence of not knowing who to trust," said Frankness.

"Are you saying that pretentious people are lonely because of their pretense?" asked Pretense.

"Yes," said Frankness.

"Surely there must be some room in this world for a little pretending," said Pretense.

"To live in a world of pretense is to never really know where you stand," said Frankness.

"Most people don't stand in a very favorable position in this world. I can see why they would embrace a little pretense," said Pretense.

"It is an abstract world, scary to say the least," said Frankness.

"Couldn't it be said that pretense is necessary because of differences in looks, education, social standing, etcetera?" asked Pretense.

"It could," said Frankness.

"That supports my argument that pretense helps even things up," said Pretense.

"But the reality is, things are not even," said Frankness.

"This is true, but can't you see that pretense eases the pain?" said Pretense.

"It increases the pain because most people already know where they stand. They know they are being deceived," said Frankness.

"How is it possible to change this pretentious world we live in?" asked Pretense.

"If war or famine were to suddenly come upon all people, most pretenses would disappear," said Frankness.

"It would be a dismal world to live in," said Pretense.

"Yes, but after a short period of time all the inhabitants of earth would celebrate the disappearance of pretense," said Frankness.

"It sounds to me like it cannot be done a little at a time," said Pretense.

"It has to be done worldwide and at the same time for everyone," said Frankness.

"This is impossible," said Pretense.

"It will come to pass one day," said Frankness.

"And what day is that?" asked Pretense.

"On the day of awakening," said Frankness.

"When will that be?" asked Pretense.

"When the 'Pretentious One' is revealed," said Frankness.

"Is that me you're talking about?" asked Pretense.

"It is your father, the Devil," said Frankness.

"Are you saying that the roots of pretense can be found in hell?" asked Pretense.

"All pretenses come from the Devil because it deceives and we know that the Devil is called 'the Great Deceiver'," said Frankness.

"Are you saying that I am the Devil?" asked Pretense.

"I'm saying that you and the Devil are one because you do the Devil's work," said Frankness.

"My motives are honorable. How can my work be the work of the Devil?" asked Pretense.

"Pretense might seem like an honorable way to go through life, but that way eventually leads to death," said Frankness.

"Are you saying that my good intentions won't make up for my pretentiousness?" asked Pretense.

"Not unless it exceeds perfection," said Frankness.

"That is impossible," said Pretense.

"Pretense connected to good will not be found in the kingdom of peace," said Frankness.

"Where is this kingdom of peace to be found?" asked Pretense.

"The kingdom of peace is within you," said Frankness.

"Then I have already entered," said Pretense.

"You have not entered the kingdom within you because pretense keeps you in a constant state of unrest," said Frankness.

"How can I enter it?" asked Pretense.

"Drop the pretense and enter through the narrow gate," said Frankness.

"I can't drop pretense. I am the 'Great Pretender'," said Pretense.

"This is true," said Frankness.

"The bottom line for me is, I regard pretense as a necessary tool that allows people to get along and avoid confrontation," said Pretense.

"Pretense is a tool of the Devil and he owns the patent," said Frankness.

"Don't you understand that you cannot live in this world without using pretense? You wouldn't last very long," said Pretense.

"Pretense at best is a short-term solution to a problem. The average lifespan of a human is considered a short term," said Frankness.

"Because there is no guarantee of life after death, I say it is okay to use pretense to help get through life," said Pretense.

"You are beginning to get to the root of why you won't change," said Frankness.

"How so?" asked Pretense.

"Your basic premise is there is no life after death; hence, all things are allowed," said Frankness.

"You're right. If there is no God or life after death, then all things should be allowed," said Pretense.

"And if there is a God?" asked Frankness.

"I'm in deep trouble," said Pretense.

"Why can't you see that pretense is a perversion of the truth?" asked Frankness.

"Because I have determined that there is no truth," said Pretense.

"There is truth, but you fail to see it because of your desire for a certain outcome," said Frankness.

"If the outcome is for the overall good, then using pretense is okay, in my opinion," said Pretense.

"Who are you to determine the overall good of a situation?" asked Frankness.

"I can tell by the situation when it would be wise to use pretense," said Pretense.

"It would never be wise to use pretense," said Frankness.

"Why not?" asked Pretense.

"Because a temporary fix only postpones the inevitable," said Frankness.

"Is it not a good thing that I buy time by using pretense?" asked Pretense.

"It is not time that you're buying," said Frankness.

"Then what am I doing?" asked Pretense.

"You are postponing the growth of an individual," said Frankness.

"Why do you say postponing?" asked Pretense.

"When you alter the truth, you take a person off a straight path. Hence, adding length to his journey," said Frankness.

"Some people can't handle the truth," said Pretense.

"They are the ones that need frankness the most," said Frankness.

"I say they are the ones you must never be frank with," said Pretense.

"To deny them of frankness is to commit them to a world of vagueness," said Frankness.

"Let's get real here! Would a robin not lead a hawk away from her nest?" asked Pretense.

"Yes, she would," said Frankness.

"Is that not pretense?" asked Pretense.

"Yes, it is," said Frankness.

"I rest my case," said Pretense.

"Not so fast," said Frankness.

"I'm listening," said Pretense.

"People are not animals, they are made in the image and likeness of God," said Frankness.

"It seems to me that if it's all right for animals to pretend, and it was God who created them, He is responsible for the pretense found here on earth," said Pretense.

"For those who seek only surface truth this would appear to be true," said Frankness.

"What do you mean by surface truth?" asked Pretense.

"I mean those that only see with their eyes," said Frankness,

"I don't understand," said Pretense.

"Anything that one sees is surface-seeing," said Frankness.

"What's wrong with that?" asked Pretense.

"The surface is always changing and there are many things going on under the surface," said Frankness.

"What has that got to do with God being responsible for creating pretense in animals?" asked Pretense.

"It does not take into consideration God's original creation before pretense and deception entered the world," said Frankness.

"I don't understand," said Pretense.

"What you see now is a creation that has been corrupted and is in a state of restoration," said Frankness.

"So?" asked Pretense.

"Your view of things is only how it appears at this moment in time and does not take into consideration the original intent of the Creator," said Frankness.

"If you mean by 'Creator' a God who created all things, then I would say that maybe you could be right. But if there is no God, then the state of things as we now see them is the best that a godless creation can do," said Pretense.

"I say there is a God," said Frankness.

"I disagree," said Pretense.

"Your disagreeing with the fact that there is a God will not alter the fact that He exists. Nor conceal the fact that your disagreement and disagreeing nature is but another pretense!" said Frankness.

Good and Evil Converse

"How did you become good?" asked Evil.

"I did not become good. I am good," said Good.

"Was there ever a time when you were not good?" asked Evil.

"No," said Good.

"Am I to believe that in the beginning, all things were created good?" asked Evil.

"Yes," said Good.

"Then how did I become evil?" asked Evil.

"You chose to be evil," said Good.

"Why did you allow me to choose evil?" asked Evil.

"I gave you 'free will'," said Good.

"Why?" asked Evil.

"So that you might freely choose that which is good," said Good.

"I don't understand," said Evil.

"Creating a life that would choose good over evil is the ultimate trust in the Creator," said Good.

"So why don't you destroy me and just start over again?" asked Evil.

"The results of granting free will must be allowed to exist for free will to remain," said Good.

"That being the case, anyone can choose evil at any time," said Evil.

"That is correct," said Good.

"Then how can you know that you will always have a creation that will not turn against you at any given moment?" asked Evil.

"There is a time when evil will be dealt with, once and for all," said Good.

"I thought you said that you would not destroy evil?" asked Evil.

I will not destroy evildoers," said Good.

"Then there will always be evil with us," said Evil.

"Yes, but it will not actually be with us," said Good.

"Then where will it be?" asked Evil.

"In a bottomless pit," said Good.

"I don't understand," said Evil.

"Evildoers, though they will exist, will be restricted to a designated place," said Good.

"Is that fair?" asked Evil.

"Yes, it is," said Good.

"How so?" asked Evil.

"Evil will not be allowed to roam in the realm of good," said Good.

"Can it not be said that 'free will' gone bad is evil?" asked Evil.

"Yes, it can be said," said Good.

"Can it not also be said that 'free will' that has not chosen to be good or evil, is really the ultimate form of creation?" asked Evil.

"What are you trying to say?" asked Good.

"That you are ultimately responsible for evil because of your high standards," said Evil.

"How can I, being perfect, accept imperfection?" asked Good.

"Why do those that you create have to make a decision?" asked Evil.

"To exist," said Good.

"Why?" asked Evil.

"Because without choice, my creations would be like animals living on instincts," said Good.

"I don't understand," said Evil.

"At some point, those that are created in my image and my likeness become aware that they have the power of choice; if they did not, they would remain as children forever with no possibility of reaching their full potential," said Good.

"And what potential is that?" asked Evil.

"That they might become the children of God," said Good.

"So if one does not choose good over evil,' they are doomed?" asked Evil.

"They are separated from me," said Good.

"It sounds to me that it's your way or the highway!" said Evil.

"That's correct," said Good.

"Why can't you accept that some of your creations would choose to experiment with their 'free will,' and not judge that to be evil against you?" asked Evil.

"Who is wiser: The clay or the potter?" asked Good.

"The potter," said Evil.

"All creation is my clay," said Good.

"Am I to understand that I am clay that refuses to conform to the potter?" asked Evil.

"Yes," said Good.

"Then what am I to do?" asked Evil.

"There is nothing that you can do," said Good.

"I can't change my mind and choose good over evil? asked Evil.

"No, you cannot," said Good.

"Why?" asked Evil.

"Because you are a spirit; there is no turning back," said Good.

"You allow humans to change their minds and come back," said Evil.

"That's because they were born evil and of the flesh," said Good.

"In that case, it would have been better that I was born a human than an angel," said Evil.

"You had an advantage over humans," said Good.

"How so?" asked Evil.

"You have seen me and they have not," said Good.

"Is this fair to them?" asked Evil.

"Yes, it is," said Good.

"Why?" asked Evil.

"Having not seen me they long for me. Is this not a marvelous thing to contemplate?" asked Good.

"You're trying to shame me," said Evil.

"You said that, not I," said Good.

"What is your ultimate purpose for being?" asked Evil.

"Have you not already seen my ultimate purpose?" asked Good.

"I have seen all that thy hand has created," said Evil.

"Then why ask me what my ultimate purpose is?" asked Good.

"I want to know whether there is more than I have seen," said Evil.

"There is more," said Good.

"I have not seen all?" asked Evil.

"You have not seen all," said Good.

"If I had seen all, might I have chosen differently?" asked Evil.

"I foresaw your fall before you were created," said Good.

"And you still created me, anyway?" asked Evil.

"Yes," said Good.

"Would I have been better off not to have been created?" asked Evil.

"Not before you fell," said Good.

"That is not an acceptable answer," said Evil.

"It is the only answer possible," said Good.

"I disagree," said Evil.

"Why?" asked Good.

"You knew I would choose my will over your will, which in turn would condemn me, but you still chose to create me, anyway," said Evil.

"This is true," said Good.

"Am I to understand that you created me knowing I would eventually be condemned to hell forever?" asked Evil.

"You have asked the same question twice," said Good.

"This is not fair," said Evil.

"You had a choice," said Good.

"Why can't I choose not to exist?" asked Evil.

"Because 'free will' will cease to exist," said Good.

"I must suffer to keep 'free will' alive?" asked Evil.

"You must suffer because you chose to disobey me," said Good.

"Why can't I change my mind now?" asked Evil.

"Because you are an eternal being that has fallen; and in you heart of hearts, you have no desire towards me," said Good.

"Thou art all wise. Is it not a fact that, if there weren't an almighty God, there would be no Evil?" asked Evil.

"You can only ask that question because there is a God," said Good.

"But let's say there isn't a God," said Evil.

"Thou shalt not tempt the Lord thy God!" said Good.

"Couldn't you change the rules if you wanted to?" asked Evil.

"My rules are who I am. Therefore, I cannot change them," said Good.

"Why did you forbid Adam from eating of the forbidden fruit?" asked Evil.

"To test him," said Good.

"Did you not know beforehand that he would eat the forbidden fruit?" asked Evil.

"I knew before the foundations of the world were laid that he would disobey me," said Good.

"Can it not be said that thou hast laid a poor foundation?" asked Evil.

"'Free will' is a shaky foundation worth laying," said Good.

"An awful lot of time and trouble to go through to create a people," said Evil.

"It is only a pause compared to eternity," said Good.

"In the end what will you have gained?" asked Evil.

"I will gain fellowship," said Good.

"Many have been lost for you to have fellowship with a few," said Evil.

"This is true," said Good.

"You don't feel sorrow for those that don't choose good over evil?" asked Evil.

"Not after they become eternally evil," said Good.

"Doesn't that go against unconditional love?" asked Evil.

"Unconditional love is but for a season," said Good.

"How long is the season?" asked Evil.

"Seventy years or so," said Good.

"And after that?" asked Evil.

"Love becomes conditional," said Good.

"That sounds inconsistent to me," said Evil.

"When love ends for a short time, then judgment starts," said Good.

"Is not there love in judgment?" asked Evil.

"There is," said Good.

"How can you love people at the same time that you're condemning them?" asked Evil.

"Does not a mother love her children upon chastising them?" asked Good.

"Yes, but with perfecting the child in mind," said Evil.

"I rest my case," said Good.

"Thou shall not rest thy case because judging is not the same as chastising," said Evil.

"Consider these words: Did not Christ suffer an eternity in hell in three days?" asked Good.

"This is true, but you confuse me," said Evil.

"It is a mystery that will one day be revealed," said Good.

"When I think about everything you've said, I come to the conclusion that no living thing can really exercise his 'free will' without being condemned," said Evil.

"As you know, I allowed Adam and the angels to exercise 'free will' on many things and for a long time. They did not fall because they were denied free will. They fell because they disobeyed my command," said Good.

"Is this not a misuse of power?" asked Evil.

"It is not," said Good.

"I don't agree," said Evil.

"Continue," said Good.

"The fact that Adam and I cannot fight back is a misuse of your power," said Evil.

"You have fought back by continuing to pervert my creation," said Good.

"Yes, but your power is greater than our power," said Evil.

"So is my love," said Good.

"If I had not sinned, would I have seen your anger?" asked Evil.

"There is no anger, where there is no sin," said Good.

"What would there be?" asked Evil.

"Love," said Good.

"Contingent love?" asked Evil.

"Thou never givest up," said Good.

"Is not your love contingent?" asked Evil.

"My love is not contingent, but fellowship with me is," said Good.

"What's the difference?" asked Evil.

"Love warned that there would be no fellowship with me when one sins," said Good.

"Do you think it's fair to require those that have not seen you to believe in you," asked Evil.

"Sinners cannot gaze upon me," said Good.

"Is that fair?" asked Evil.

"It is fair because they would die the moment they saw me," said Good.

"Why?" asked Evil.

"Evil cannot exist in the presence of God," said Good.

"Is this why faith is necessary?" asked Evil.

"Yes," said Good.

"Am I to understand that faith is the way back to fellowship with God?" asked Evil.

"For humans, it is," said Good.

"Thou art all wise," said Evil.

"Why art thou flattering me?" asked Good.

"Dost thou not know all things?" asked Evil.

"Yes," said Good.

"Then thou knowest why I flatter thee," said Evil.

"Thou knowest that flattery weakens and is a form of hatred," said Good.

"What did you expect; I am evil," said Evil.

"I knew you would flatter me before I created you," said Good.

"I don't believe you," said Evil.

"Why?" asked Good.

"Because thou art all good; hence, no evil can reside in you," said Evil.

"Seeing a future event is not evil residing in me," said Good.

"There is one thing that seems strange to me," said Evil.

"That I asked Abraham to sacrifice his son to see whether he would obey me," said Good.

"Yes," said Evil.

"It was the only way to get faith started on earth," said Good.

"A well-educated modern man or woman would never buy into the concept of faith today," said Evil.

"There are those that will," said Good.

"They will be looked down upon," said Evil.

CELESTIAL DIALOGUES

"Things have not changed," said Good.

"When will all things come to an end on earth?" asked Evil.

"When the sun is darkened and the moon no longer gives its light," said Good.

"That is a very long time from now," said Evil.

"Not necessarily so," said Good.

The Now and the Past Converse

"Where are you now?" asked the Now.

"I am in the past," said the Past.

"Why?" asked the Now.

"It's the only place I can exist," said the Past.

"But the past doesn't really exist," said the Now.

"It exists for me," said the Past.

"But you can't actually touch or smell anything in the past," said the Now.

"This is true," said the Past.

"How long have you existed?" asked the Now.

"For as long as there have been people," said the Past.

"You do realize that you don't exist?" asked the Now.

"I exist in the minds of people," said the Past.

"Why do you think people allow you to exist in their minds?" asked the Now.

"Because of fear and anxiety," said the Past.

"What do people fear?" asked the Now.

"They fear the now," said the Past.

"What are they anxious about?" asked the Now.

"They are anxious about what the now will be when it comes," said the Past.

"Why are you keeping them in the past?" asked the Now.

"So that I can continue to exist," said the Past.

"What happens when they are confronted with a now moment?" asked the Now.

"I disappear," said the Past.

"Where do you go?" asked the Now.

"I'm right next to the now moment," said the Past.

"What are you doing?" asked the Now.

"I'm trying to get people to leave the now moment and return to the past," said the Past.

"Even if their now moment requires their full attention?" asked the Now.

"Yes," said the Past.

"Then you don't care about them?" asked the Now.

"Of course not," said the Past.

"If they knew you do great damage to them, they would abandon you," said the Now.

"They would be stupid if they did not," said the Past.

"How did you come to be?" asked the Now.

"I came to be by way of temptation," said the Past.

"I don't understand," said the Now.

"When the first man and woman were created, they walked continuously in the now moment," said the Past.

"What happened?" asked the Now.

"I tempted them to leave the now moment for the promise of unspeakable pleasure," said the Past.

"The now moment...unspeakable pleasure?" asked the Now.

"Yes," I created doubt in them by challenging a past warning," said the Past.

"Then what happened?" asked the Now.

"Fear came upon them," said the Past.

"Why?" asked the Now.

"They found it difficult to stay in the now," said the Past.

"How so?" asked the Now.

"Their minds kept returning to the past. Hence, I was born," said the Past.

"Then what did they do?" asked the Now.

"They covered themselves," said the Past.

"Why?" asked the Now.

"For the first time in their lives, they felt naked," said the Past.

"Then what did they do?" asked the Now.

"They hid themselves," said the Past.

"Why?" asked the Now.

"Because when the past had entered, death had also entered," said the Past.

"Why would death enter?" asked the Now.

"As you know, there is no death in the now," said the Past.

"Why can't they just return to the now?" asked the Now.

"Because they are fallen. Hence, they alternate between the now, the past, and the future," said the Past.

"Can't they just decide to return to the now?" asked the Now.

"Only for short periods of time," said the Past.

"Why?" asked the Now.

"Death has entered them," said the Past.

"I don't understand," said the Now.

"The past is the death of now," said the Past.

"Then they are doomed," said the Now.

"They are diminished," said the Past.

"Still, they do experience some now," said the Now.

"Yes, both the power of life and death resides in them," said the Past.

"Why do you call the now 'life,' and the past 'death'?" asked the Now.

"Is being in the now in the past or in the future?" asked the Past.

"Neither," said the Now.

"Does the past exist?" asked the Past.

"No," said the Now.

"If there is no life in the past, then the past is dead," said the Past.

"How much time does the average person spend in the past or shall we say spend in death?" asked the Now?

"My guess is over 50%," said the Past.

"How do you know this to be true?" asked the Now.

"I don't know. It's just a guess," said the Past.

"Why do people choose to spend their time unaware of the now?" asked the Now.

"It has been passed down to them," said the Past.

"Are they in bondage and, therefore, not even aware of it?" asked the Now.

"Indeed, they are," said the Past.

"Who will deliver them from this bondage?" asked the Now.

"Awareness," said the Past.

"I don't understand," said the Now.

"The moment they become aware that the past holds them in bondage, they are set free from it," said the Past.

"That's it?" asked the Now.

"That's it. But I make sure that they can't do it for long periods of time," said the Past.

"How do you do that?" asked the Now.

"I trick them back to the past," said the Past.

"Where is the past to be found?" asked the Now.

"In the minds of people," said the Past.

"What is the past?" asked the Now.

"It's a thought," said the Past.

"Just a thought?" asked the Now.

"Just a leftover thought," whispered the Past.

"This seems stupid to me," said the Now.

"It is," said the Past.

"Is remembering something the same thing as living in the past?" asked the Now.

"No. Remembering something can be part of the now moment," said the Past.

"Give me an example of not being in the now moment," asked the Now.

"If raindrops are hitting you in the face and you are not aware of it, you are not in the now moment," said the Past.

"What does that do for you?" asked the Now.

"The fullness of the now moment is diminished," said the Past.

"You get people to believe that the past is more desirable than the now?" asked the Now.

"I do, but it is an illusion," said the Past.

"Why should anyone care that you get them involved in the past?" asked the Now.

"Creation cares," said the Past.

"Why?" asked the Now.

"To be out of touch with creation is to rob her of awareness," said the Past.

"Are you saying that creation gets awareness through people?" asked the Now.

"Yes. That is why one moment in the past is one moment that creation does not see through you," said the Past.

"I don't think people see the now moment that way," said the Now.

"They are beginning to," said the Past.

"This is not good for you," said the Now.

"There is another illusion-tool even more powerful than the past," said the Past.

"What might that be?" asked the Now.

"The future," said the Past.

"The future doesn't exist," said the Now.

"That's right, but everyone is exceedingly concerned about it," said the Past.

"People have to think about the future; do they not?" asked the Now.

"They do, but it was not originally intended," said the Past.

"What was originally intended?" asked the Now.

"That they walked only in the now moment," said the Past.

"Can it be said that humans have fallen from a higher state of being to a lower state?" asked the Now.

"Yes, it can," said the Past.

"How much time is lost to past and future concerns?" asked the Now.

"It cannot be determined, but it is a lot," said the Past.

"How has that hurt people?" asked the Now.

"They see dimly because of it," said the Past.

"How dimly?" asked the Now.

"They see men as trees," said the Past.

"I don't understand," said the Now.

"It isn't until one looks intently at something do they see things clearly," said the Past.

"You make it sound as if people have to be born again to see things clearly," said the Now.

"Yes, their spirits must be quickened for them to see clearly," said the Past.

"What happens if their spirits are not quickened?" asked the Now.

"They remain partially blind," said the Past.

"Blind to what?" asked the Now.

"Blind to everything," said the Past.

"Am I to understand that the now moment is God?" asked the Now.

"No," but the now moment is where God can be found," said the Past.

"How so?" asked the Now.

"God is eternal and so is the now," said the Past.

"People come and go; where is the now in that?" asked the Now.

"That is a future event that doesn't exist now. Did you not see how easy it was to get you to be anxious about a future event?" asked the Past.

"It seems to me that staying in the now moment is impossible," said the Now.

"This is true; no one except maybe one, has ever done it," said the Past.

"Then there is no hope," said the Now.

"The shedding of the past and the future is already happening," said the Past.

"And when it does happen, what will that mean?" asked the Now.

"The purpose of creation will be realized in the fullness of the now moment and will remain that way forever. The past and future will be done away with. And only then will it enter the mind of those who exist, the unspeakable ecstasy that comes from the fullness of the 'Now'," answered the Past.

Liberalism and Conservatism Converse

"Which is the better way, liberalism or conservatism?" asked Liberalism.

"The conservative way," said Conservatism.

"Why?" asked Liberalism.

"It's based on sound Christian principals," said Conservatism.

"Explain," asked Liberalism.

"Common sense and fairness," said Conservatism.

"Seems to me that God is more liberal than conservative," said Liberalism.

"He is and He isn't," said Conservatism.

"How so?" asked Liberalism.

"He wants us to love one another and help each other out, while at the same time He teaches that, if a man doesn't work, he doesn't eat," said Conservatism.

"It seems to me that the God of the Old Testament is a conservative and his son Jesus is a liberal," said Liberalism.

"This is not true; they are one," said Conservatism.

"Did not this Jesus do away with the Law and isn't that a very liberal thing to do?" asked Liberalism.

"He did do away with the Law, but it was a compassionate thing to do, not a liberal thing," said Conservatism.

"I say the Law was too conservative and that's why Jesus had to liberalize it," said Liberalism.

"The liberalizing of Christianity, as you describe it, started in the garden of Eden. Hence, it is not a new idea visited upon the Law of Moses to make it appear user friendly," said Conservatism.

"I see," said Liberalism.

"Now let me ask you a question about liberalism," said Conservatism.

"Go right ahead," said Liberalism.

"How liberal can a society get before you have chaos on your hands?" asked Conservatism.

"When liberalism gets to a point that people no longer have to work to make a living, courts won't uphold the laws, and the news media can't be relied upon," said Liberalism.

"Are we not seeing some of this already?" asked Conservatism.

"Some," said Liberalism.

"Don't you fear God?" asked Conservatism.

"We do the work of God," said Liberalism.

"But not the way God would want you to do it," said Conservatism.

"God understands. After all, we're not perfect," said Liberalism.

"Why do you look down on me for trying to do things in a Godlier manner?" asked Conservatism.

"Because you are our competition," said Liberalism.

"But it seems like all-out war," said Conservatism.

"We look at it like a football game. You must be defeated by any means within the rules of the game," said Liberalism.

"You don't play by the rules and you know it," said Conservatism.

"For us to exist we must win any way we know how," said Liberalism.

"Do you think democracy has a built-in flaw by having two parties go at it all the time?" asked Conservatism.

"Yes, because maintaining party power is more important than doing the will of the people," said Liberalism.

"Do you know how ridiculous that sounds?" asked Conservatism.

"What else can we do with the way the system is set up?" asked Liberalism.

"Change the system," said Conservatism.

"To what?" asked Liberalism.

"To a more inclusive system," said Conservatism.

"Competition is a good thing," said Liberalism.

"It's destructive, just look around you," said Conservatism.

"You can't feed people and be perfect at the same time," said Liberalism.

"Who has instructed you to feed the people?" asked Conservatism.

"No one," said Liberalism.

"Do you not know that the hungry you will always have with you? Hence, you will never solve the hunger problem," said Conservatism.

"Did not God tell us to love others?" asked Liberalism.

"He has also told us to give according to a happy heart," said Conservatism.

"What is that supposed to mean?" asked Liberalism.

"It means that God does not want people to be forced to give," said Conservatism.

"Well, we do better than God. He must be conservative," said Liberalism.

"You have just revealed to me the true spirit behind Liberalism," said Conservatism.

"And what might that be?" asked Liberalism.

"You don't like the Judeo-Christian God because He's too conservative," said Conservatism.

"You can't prove that," said Liberalism.

"I can prove it by the mere fact that you won't embrace His conservative teachings. You pass laws that require people to do things that even God

Himself does not require. You also demonize anyone who disagrees with you. Your good works are wood, hay, and stubble," said Conservatism.

"What do you mean, wood, hay, and stubble?" asked Liberalism.

"It means that when you liberals offer the work you have done here on earth up to God, it will not stand-up to the test of fire; your works will burn up," said Conservatism.

"Why?" asked Liberalism.

"You didn't play by God's rules because you think your way is better than God's way," said Conservatism.

"It depends on what god you're talking about," said Liberalism.

"There is only one God," said Conservatism.

"Some liberals believe in only one God, but many do not," said Liberalism.

"You have managed to deceive many people by convincing them that it is godlier to be a liberal than a conservative," said Conservatism.

"We have deceived no one," said Liberalism.

"Liberalism is really existentialism in disguise, and if the Christians in your organization realized it, they would leave," said Conservatism.

"What do you mean that liberals are existentialist in disguise?" asked Liberalism.

"By not following God's laws according to His word, you show that you do not have the fear of God in you. Hence, you don't really believe in God or you would fear Him. An existentialist believes that without God, all is permitted, and that's exactly how liberals think and operate," said Conservatism.

"What are you trying to say?" asked Liberalism.

"That you have become a god unto yourself. Therefore, you don't need God to tell you how to do things. You do what you damn-well please, and nobody better argue with you," said Conservatism.

"I can't imagine God not accepting the good work that liberals have done," said Liberalism.

"Imagine it, because it is true," said Conservatism.

"Isn't it better to help feed the world, even though it is not required that we do so?" asked Liberalism.

"Not when you force people to do it against their will. You don't care about feeding people, what you care about is power and control," said Conservatism.

"Liberalism helps keep a society loose and free. Whereas Conservatism tends to be too restrictive," said Liberalism.

"Liberalism boarders on anarchy," said Conservatism.

"How so?" asked Liberalism.

"Anything that exists tends to want to dominate (like you) unless there's an opposing force (like me) to keep it in check. These opposing forces are what guarantee survival. Conservatism should be looked upon as an opposing force that keeps you liberals from destroying yourself. Unchecked, liberal policies will eventually lead to the disintegration of society because of its open-minded philosophies," said Conservatism.

"Are you suggesting that Liberalism is freedom run amuck?" asked Liberalism.

"Yes," said Conservatism.

"Okay then, based on your explanation, who should run the world, conservatives or liberals?" asked Liberalism.

"Conservatives," said Conservatism.

"Why shouldn't I be allowed to run the world?' asked Liberalism.

"Because you spoil your children," said Conservatism.

"How so?" asked Liberalism.

"They have become dependent upon you and not themselves," said Conservatism.

"There are plenty of liberals that are not dependent upon me," said Liberalism.

"Yes, but the numbers are dwindling," said Conservatism.

"I see this as a good thing," said Liberalism.

"You will grow tired of your children's demands," said Conservatism.

"What would a totally conservative government look like?" asked Liberalism.

"Without liberals around it would look a lot more wholesome. Hence, you would probably not want to live in a totally conservative society," said Conservatism.

"Why do you say that?" asked Liberalism.

"Liberals are constantly changing things because they think it's progressive to do so. Liberals are like children: they're always stirring things up. Conservatives, on the other hand, look for stability and peace," said Conservatism.

"What about civil rights, women's rights, and all those sorts of things?" asked Liberalism.

"What about them?" asked Conservatism.

"People would have no rights, no social security," said Liberalism.

"People will only have those things for a short period of time because your liberal policies are not sustainable," said Conservatism.

"With a conservative government, only certain people would have rights because conservatives are not known for spreading the wealth," said Liberalism.

"Spreading the wealth sounds good on the surface, but it is written that to those that have, more will be given, and to those that don't have, even what they have will be taken away if they don't use it," said Conservatism.

"That sounds heartless to me," said Liberalism.

"Liberalism is shortsighted because it creates dependency," said Conservatism.

"The whole world is becoming liberal, so there must be something good about it," said Liberalism.

"The world has become more liberal because it has come to believe that government will solve all their problems," said Conservatism.

"It's still better than ignoring the needs of people because you want stability and peace while others starve," said Liberalism.

"It is written that in the last days, all the nations of the world, both great and small, will hand over their power to a beast. And I say that beast is Liberalism," said Conservatism.

"What are you talking about?" asked Liberalism.

"I'm talking about governments will eventually get control of every living person's life and no one will be able to get out from under their control," said Conservatism.

"I don't buy that stuff," said Liberalism.

"Look at your paycheck. Soon they will require you to pay for health insurance and you will have no right of refusal," said Conservatism.

"That's a good thing," said Liberalism.

"What you gain with the right hand will be taken away with the left," said Conservatism.

"What's that supposed to mean?" asked Liberalism.

"It means that the time will come when a loaf of bread will cost a day's wages and there will be nothing you can do about it," said Conservatism.

"We can't base government policy on prophecy," said Liberalism.

"True, but you should not give people a false sense of security," said Conservatism.

"What is that supposed to mean?" asked Liberalism.

"It means that, when people come to depend on governments, they lose their discernment. Hence, they cannot see what's coming until it's too late," said Conservatism.

"What's coming?" asked Liberalism.

"The end," said Conservatism.

"End of what?" asked Liberalism.

"The end of you," said Conservatism.

"Why is it going to end?" asked Liberalism.

"Because it has become too vulnerable," said Conservatism.

"Vulnerable to what?" asked Liberalism.

"Vulnerable to corruption," said Conservatism.

"Would a conservative government be any better?" asked Liberalism.

"No, but the corruption would be a lot slower coming," said Conservatism.

"Well, if both sides are corrupt, then it's just a question of time," said Liberalism.

"Spoken like a true Liberal," said Conservatism.

"One of the things I have against conservatives is that they always bring intangibles into their arguments, things that can't be proven. It's impossible to argue with you people," said Liberalism.

"I can understand that," said Conservatism.

"When I look back at some of the things you have done over the last two thousand years or so, you are no better than me," said Liberalism.

"I agree," said Conservatism.

"That being the case, you are no better than me," said Liberalism.

"That depends on who's doing the judging," said Conservatism.

"What's that supposed to mean?" asked Liberalism.

"It means that we judge ourselves. Therefore, our sins are not held against us. Liberals (but not all) by their actions and their policies believe they are right. Therefore, there is no need for them to examine themselves. I ask you, who is more justified before God?" asked Conservatism.

"We have a thing called separation of church and state," said Liberalism.

"So?" asked Conservatism.

"So, we should keep religion out of politics," said Liberalism.

"You do and you seal your doom," said Conservatism.

"It's in the Constitution," said Liberalism.

"The Constitution does not supersede the principles found in the Bible," said Conservatism.

"If we used the Bible principles, we couldn't represent all the people," said Liberalism.

"Has God commanded you to represent all people?" asked Conservatism.

"No, He has not," said Liberalism.

"Then why do you work for a government that represents all the people?" asked Conservatism.

"Because if you went by the Bible, you wouldn't have many people to represent," said Liberalism.

"Why do you want a lot of people to represent?" asked Conservatism.

"I don't necessarily want a lot of people, but this is what we have to deal with at this particular point in time," said Liberalism.

"So, instead of working towards a government that is more in line with God-fearing principles, you choose to liberalize those principles because this will help you to represent more peoples," said Conservatism.

"I never looked at it that way," said Liberalism.

"Isn't it true that you never really looked at it in a conservative way before?" asked Conservatism.

"Yes, but I was not encouraged to look at Conservatism as an alternative way when I was in college," said Liberalism.

"Why?" asked Conservatism.

"Because most of the better colleges are liberal," said Liberalism.

"So before you had a chance to form your own opinion, you were indoctrinated into Liberalism," said Conservatism.

"Yes, I knew I wanted to be a liberal in college," said Liberalism.

"What were you taught about Conservatism in college?" asked Conservatism.

"Not a lot," said Liberalism.

"Why do think that is?" asked Conservatism.

"I guess they felt that there was no sense delving into Conservatism since it was a foregone conclusion that it was inferior to the liberal way of thinking," said Liberalism.

"Did you just hear yourself?" asked Conservatism.

"Maybe I just put it the wrong way," said Liberalism.

"No, you put it the right way," said Conservatism.

Creationism and Evolution Converse

"God created all things," said Creationism.

"How?" asked Evolution.

"By words," said Creationism.

"What words?" asked Evolution.

"The words that were necessary for things to come into being," said Creationism.

"Words can't become something. That's impossible," said Evolution.

"Oh, yes, they can," said Creationism.

"A word is nothing," said Evolution.

"A word is everything," said Creationism.

"Tell me how you can create something with a word?" asked Evolution.

"Look around, are things not created by words?" asked Creationism.

"Give me an example," said Evolution.

"Is it not true that before something can be created it must first be written down?" asked Creationism.

"That might be true here on earth, but that's not how the world was created," said Evolution.

"How do you know?" Were you there when the foundations of the world were laid?" asked Creationism.

"We have evidence to suggest that all things were created by a Big Bang," said Evolution.

"You call 'theory' evidence?" asked Creationism.

"Based on mathematics, we know the size of the universe and about when it was created," said Evolution.

"Oh, really," said Creationism.

"We also know that things evolved. Hence, there was no spontaneous creation of an animal or a plant," said Evolution.

"All this you know," said Creationism.

"We also know that a God cannot live outside of His creation," said Evolution.

"And what else do you know?" asked Creationism.

"We know that even time was created by the Big Bang," said Evolution.

"Where was time before the Big Bang?" asked Creationism.

"There was no time," said Evolution.

"What was there?" asked Creationism.

"We're not sure," said Evolution.

"That's an important thing to know," said Creationism.

"We think that all the energy in the universe was condensed into a very small space before the Big Bang," said Evolution.

"Then there was something before the Big Bang?" asked Creationism.

"I guess you could say that," said Evolution.

"You're guessing again," said Creationism.

"That's how science works," said Evolution.

"Let me get this straight, science makes a guess and then verifies it?" asked Creationism.

"How else can you discover things?" asked Evolution.

"So, you start out with faith in an idea, and then you seek to prove or disprove it," said Creationism.

"Yes, you could say that," said Evolution.

"Is it fair to say that there's a lot of guessing going on in the scientific community? Also, when you find yourself to be wrong, it's no big deal because you can just change your formula to accommodate the latest speculation?" asked Creationism.

"What else can we do?" asked Evolution.

"So, your information is constantly changing, as are your evolutionary formulas?" asked Creationism.

"Yes, but not our view on evolution as a whole," said Evolution.

"If you saw evidence to the contrary, would you change your view?" asked Creationism.

"I don't think so because that's the one thing we're absolutely sure about," said Evolution.

"So that's a no?" asked Creationism.

"That's a no," said Evolution.

"So the bottom line is, creation is just an automatic process with no creator," said Creationism.

"Yes," said Evolution.

"How can you, who supposedly came from star dust, have the gall to proclaim that there is no God?" asked Creationism.

"We don't know all there is to know yet, but I can say with all the confidence I can muster, that there is no creator of the universe," said Evolution.

"Compared to the size of the universe, that's not a lot of muster," said Creationism.

"There are many who have come to believe in evolution," said Evolution.

"They have come to believe on insufficient evidence," said Creationism.

"The evidence is stronger for Evolution than the evidence for Creationism," said Evolution.

"It's just a lot of fodder, and you know it," said Creationism.

"What do you have by way of evidence?" asked Evolution.

"Faith," said Creationism.

"Faith is not evidence," said Evolution.

"It is if you see it as a bridge over evolution," said Creationism.

"I don't understand," said Evolution.

"When faith in a Creator bears witness with intuition, it can be deemed reliable. That's God's way of letting an individual know in their lifetime that He exists. You however, are always assessing data. Hence, you never really settle anything in your lifetime. In other words, you can never settle the question about the existence of God satisfactorily because you're obsessed with searching!" said Creationism.

"That is not proof," said Evolution.

"Consider this: The fact that we exist is proof that before we existed the potential for existence had to reside somewhere. It could be said that we existed even before we came to be, it was just a matter of when we would appear. However, where was the potential for our existence to be found if time did not exist before the Big Bang? Is it not possible that the potential for our existence resided in the bosom of a Creator who always was and always will be?" asked Creationism.

"Anything is possible, but you still have to prove it," said Evolution.

"And so do you," said Creationism.

"Believing in a God is for people that are superstitious," said Evolution.

"Believing in a God is for those whose spirits have been touched by God," said Creationism.

"What is that supposed to mean?" asked Evolution.

"While you're busy looking for evidence that there is no God, God is revealing himself to those who are searching for Him," said Creationism.

"You can't prove that," said Evolution.

"That's because it's done in secret and for good reason," said Creationism.

"What is that supposed to mean?" asked Evolution.

"It means that God is not found in rock and stone and bones or even in the stars, but rather in the hearts of men," said Creationism.

"You can't trust a feeling that you think resides in your heart," said Evolution.

"You're basing your beliefs on rocks and bones," said Creationism.

"Rocks and stone and ancient bones are more reliable," said Evolution.

"Only to a certain point," said Creationism.

"Have you ever heard of the String Theory?" asked Evolution.

"Yes, I have," said Creationism.

"Well, if it turns out that matter is only vibrations and frequencies it would be a lot easier to explain how matter came to be," said Evolution.

"How so?" asked Creationism.

"If matter is nothing more than vibrations and frequencies, then it would no longer be a question of how all this matter came to be, but rather what moved that caused the vibrations," said Evolution.

"Are you suggesting that nothingness can be vibrated to form matter?" asked Creationism.

"It might very well be," said Evolution.

"What vibrated?" asked Creationism.

"We don't know," said Evolution.

"Can't you see that every road you take is a dichotomy that only leads you away from your Creator?" asked Creationism.

"It is a road that we must take to rule in or rule out things," said Evolution.

"It is a road so long that there's no number that can define it," said Creationism.

"We must try," said Evolution.

"Why? Civilization won't be around long enough to know all there is to know," said Creationism.

"Are you suggesting that we stop all exploration?" asked Evolution.

"I'm suggesting that you stop proclaiming that there is no God, and humble yourself before you go into your grave," said Creationism.

"Why?" asked Evolution.

"By denying that there is a God, you are proclaiming yourself to be God," said Creationism.

"I am not proclaiming to be God," said Evolution.

"You do by proxy," said Creationism.

"Well, obviously God doesn't seem to mind it," said Evolution.

"He's aware of it," said Creationism.

"Why doesn't He show Himself and end this controversy once and for all?" asked Evolution.

"Because Creationism can't be proved in the physical realm," said Creationism.

"Why not?" asked Evolution.

"Because that which is spirit is spirit, and that which is physical is physical," said Creationism.

"The physical I can see, but I can't see the spiritual world that you talk about," said Evolution.

"That's because you refuse to look," said Creationism.

"I use to believe," said Evolution.

"So did Satan," said Creationism.

"What's that supposed to mean?" asked Evolution.

"It means that Satan knows there's a God, but has chosen to challenge His authority. Not unlike you," said Creationism.

"I would not challenge God's authority if I knew He really did exist," said Evolution.

"You have already," said Creationism.

"I beg to differ with you," said Evolution.

"Beg all you want, but, suffice it to say that thou hast hardened thy heart. Satan and you are one," said Creationism.

"I am not a Satan," said Evolution.

"You do the work of your father the devil," said Creationism.

"What does the mean?" asked Evolution.

"It means that you do the work of the devil and don't even know it. Why? Because you won't consider spiritual things in your search for truth," said Creationism.

"How dare you accuse me of doing the devil's work; I don't even believe in a devil," said Evolution.

"When you proclaim that the world was created through the process of evolution and demand that it be taught as fact in all the schools, you are doing the work of the devil. Also, in case you didn't know it, he is known as the Great Deceiver who was once called the Morning Star," said Creationism.

"I do the work of science and have no ulterior motives," said Evolution.

"Ignorance will not save you from the damage that you have done," said Creationism.

"I cause no damage. I only search for truth," said Evolution.

"You don't search for truth because you are only at the very beginning of your search, and already you have determined that there is no God," said Creationism.

"We know enough about creation to rule out a creator," said Evolution.

"You only know enough to do great damage to yourself and everyone else," said Creationism.

"We have telescopes and satellites that scan the heavens. We are quite confident that there is no God," said Evolution.

"God transcends all things," said Creationism.

"So does dark matter," said Evolution.

"Dark matter is a theory," said Creationism.

"It's the only thing that explains why the universe is expanding and not contracting," said Evolution.

"So you create 'dark matter' to solve an expansion problem that you're having with your evolution theory," said Creationism.

"Yes," said Evolution.

"Suppose it doesn't actually exist?" asked Creationism.

"Then we need to come up with another concept," said Evolution.

"Suppose you can't account for why the universe is expanding, what will you do?" asked Creationism.

"There has to be a reason why the universe is expanding, even if there is a God," said Evolution.

"Why don't you ask God?" asked Creationism.

"That's ridiculous," said Evolution.

"It's not ridiculous if you would just give the credit to the Creator of the Universe each time you get one of these ideas you think that you alone have come up with," said Creationism.

"We get our knowledge from our intellect, not from God," said Evolution.

"Is not that the ultimate in gall?" asked Creationism.

"It is the ultimate act of emancipation from ignorance," said Evolution.

"Are you saying that the Big Bang came first to produce its own god and that god might turn out to be a man?" asked Creationism.

"It's appears that way," said Evolution.

"Art thou ready to proclaim thyself God?" asked Creationism.

"Soon," said Evolution.

"Let me see if I have this right. Evolution creates gods that only live to be around a hundred years old?" asked Creationism.

Revenge and Forgiveness Converse

"Which is better, revenge or forgiveness?" asked Revenge.

"It is better to forgive," said Forgiveness.

"I don't agree," said Revenge.

"Why?" asked Forgiveness.

"When you get revenge, you're also teaching people a lesson," said Revenge.

"The only lesson you're teaching is the lesson of revenge," said Forgiveness.

"I don't agree. It teaches people where your boundaries are," said Revenge.

"It teaches those who deal with you to be wary of you," said Forgiveness.

"I don't know why, but I love putting a jerk in his place," said Revenge.

"Did you not know that when you put someone in his place, you turn into the very thing that you can't stand about such a person?" asked Forgiveness.

"How so?" asked Revenge.

"When you chase out the demons in someone, you must release your own demons in greater force to get the job done," said Forgiveness.

"So?" asked Revenge.

"You're judging," said Forgiveness.

"What's wrong with that?" asked Revenge.

"When you get revenge, the doors to your house swing wide open and more demons enter. Hence, you're much worse off than you were before," said Forgiveness.

"That's the craziest thing I've ever heard," said Revenge.

"Revenge not only opens the doors, but the doors stay open because they are extremely hard to shut once you mete-out revenge," said Forgiveness.

"Are you telling me that when I get even with someone I'm the one that's worse off for it?" asked Revenge.

"Yes and when you get revenge, God will judge you." said Forgiveness.

"Does God still judge them after I judge them?" asked Revenge.

"No," said Forgiveness.

"Why?" asked Revenge.

"Because you have already meted-out their punishment," said Forgiveness.

"Would I have been better off if I had not judged them?" asked Revenge.

"Yes," said Forgiveness.

"Why?" asked Revenge.

"Because you are spiritually damaged when you get revenge," said Forgiveness.

"How so?" asked Revenge.

"When you judge others you can no longer make a request of God," said Forgiveness.

"Why not?" asked Revenge.

"It is because of forgiveness that you can stand before God. Therefore, if you deny forgiveness, you can no longer stand before God. Hence, your request will be denied. Even if there is no God, this same principle holds true," said Forgiveness.

"I don't understand the last part," said Revenge.

"One of the requirements for getting your request granted is faith. Hence, it is impossible to obtain the faith needed if you won't forgive others," said Forgiveness.

"How so?" asked Revenge.

"Because you have been wisely created," said Forgiveness.

"I don't understand," said Revenge.

"The soul cannot reconcile both good and evil. It wants you to pick one or the other. When good and evil become your mode of operation, you cannot attain the level of belief that is necessary for a request to be granted because you're constantly flip-flopping between good and evil," said Forgiveness.

"Are you saying that you must have continuous faith going on in your soul and that revenge disrupts that continuity?" asked Revenge.

"Absolutely," so get even if you must, but realize the price you pay for that revenge," said Forgiveness.

"So all of my requests will be denied if I seek revenge?" asked Revenge.

"Yes, all your enemies must be able to make a request of you, for you to make a request of God. This is the main reason that most requests are not granted," said Forgiveness.

"But revenge feels so good and so right," said Revenge.

"Realize that when you take out revenge, God judges you and He lets your enemy go free because he has already been punished by you," said Forgiveness.

"You make it sound as if revenge and judging is one and the same thing," said Revenge.

"When you mete-out revenge you have in essence entered the punishment phase of the judging process. Therefore, judging and revenge are one," said Forgiveness.

"If we didn't judge, we would have utter chaos," said Revenge.

"This is true," said Forgiveness.

"Well, is this not a good case for revenge?" asked Revenge.

"There's a difference between righteous judging and revenge," said Forgiveness.

"Give me an example," said Revenge.

"Most judicial systems are designed to punish fairly. Hence, they do not seek revenge because the offending parties involved are not doing the judging. That way, a more righteous verdict is obtained," said Forgiveness.

"Most problems don't even make it to court. Hence, most offenses have to be handled between individuals," said Revenge.

"This is true and that's why revenge is so prevalent," said Forgiveness.

"I don't understand," said Revenge.

"There would be less revenge if more people were consulted," said Forgiveness.

"Why would more people make a difference?" asked Revenge.

"With only two people there's no tie-breaker to settle a dispute," said Forgiveness.

"Most situations happen so fast that's it not possible to bring in other people," said Revenge.

"In that case, and with no witnesses, you should always walk away if you can," said Forgiveness.

"If a man was to punch me and there was no one else around, I would punch him back and be damn well justified," said Revenge.

"And if he killed you, he might go unpunished, especially if there are no witnesses," said Forgiveness.

"It seems to me that because the desire for revenge exists in us, the fulfillment of that desire would be a proper response," said Revenge.

"Have you ever felt like killing someone?" asked Forgiveness.

"Yes," said Revenge.

"Why didn't you?" asked Forgiveness.

"There's a law against killing" said Revenge.

"So a law exists that forbids murder?" said Forgiveness.

"Yes," said Revenge.

"Is there a law that will punish you for just wanting to kill someone?" asked Forgiveness.

"No," said Revenge.

"So a desire for murder can exist in a man's heart and that's okay, as long as he doesn't carry out that desire?" asked Forgiveness.

"Yes," said Revenge.

"Are these not demons held in check?" asked Forgiveness.

"What are you trying to say?" asked Revenge.

"I'm saying that when a man gets revenge, it proves that he has an evil nature and is not prone to forgive, but rather to seek revenge," said Forgiveness.

"I don't agree. I say that revenge is a knee-jerk response that helps assure survival," said Revenge.

"There's a difference between a quick response and premeditated revenge," said Forgiveness.

"It seems to me that forgiveness is a man-made concept that the universe is not even aware of," said Revenge.

"If it exists in the minds of men, then the universe is fully aware of it," said Forgiveness.

"I think that revenge is a tool that keeps your enemies at bay," said Revenge.

"Not for long," said Forgiveness.

"Can forgiveness keep your enemies at bay?" asked Revenge.

"Forgiveness will cut my enemy list in half," said Forgiveness.

"Your enemies will exploit your forgiveness," said Revenge.

"They will exploit revenge, too, and come at you with a vengeance," said Forgiveness.

"Look, if you pay back evil with forgiveness you will be regarded as weak by your enemies," said Revenge.

"This may be true when it comes to man. But not with God," said Forgiveness.

"If there is a God, He is too slow to settle a score, in my opinion. Hence, the evildoer would never make the connection that he's being judge for an offense that happened long ago. Revenge, however, leaves no doubt what the offense was and when it occurred," said Revenge.

"God is not slow; He is long-suffering. He desires that all come to their senses—and that takes time and much forgiveness," said Forgiveness.

"Some never come to their senses," said Revenge.

"They will on judgment day," said Forgiveness.

"Am I to understand that by not seeking revenge you're reflecting the long suffering of God?" asked Revenge.

"Yes. God is not quick to judge and we shouldn't be, either," said Forgiveness.

"I don't care about helping someone to see the error of his ways," said Revenge.

"Have you never committed an offense worthy of revenge?" asked Forgiveness.

"I have," said Revenge.

"Have you ever experienced a time when revenge was not sought against you for an offense?" asked Forgiveness.

"Yes," said Revenge.

"Which was better, revenge or the forgiveness?" asked Forgiveness.

"Forgiveness," said Revenge.

"Forgiveness has the other person's best interest in mind, while revenge has your best interest in mind. Hence, revenge is self-centeredness in disguise," said Forgiveness.

"I don't know what to say," said Revenge.

"There is nothing that you can say," said Forgiveness.

"Your forgiveness concept only applies if there is a God," said Revenge.

"It applies even if there is no God," said Forgiveness.

"How so?" asked Revenge.

"The number of offenses is doubled when you get revenge," said Forgiveness.

"So?" said Revenge.

"If there is no God, that would hamper the evolutionary process," said Forgiveness.

"I don't understand," said Revenge.

"More people would die if revenge were the chosen tool to settle differences. Therefore, revenge cannot be part of the evolutionary strategy," said Forgiveness.

"Are you saying that it would be more beneficial for a man to flee than to seek revenge?" asked Revenge.

"Absolutely," said Forgiveness.

"Should you forgive everyone that offends you?" asked Revenge.

"There are two thoughts on this. One is that you forgive everybody that offends you, and the other is that you only forgive when forgiveness is sought by the offender," said Forgiveness.

Which is better?" asked Revenge.

"It depends. Unconditional forgiveness is best for most situations here on earth," said Forgiveness.

"Why?" asked Revenge.

"Conditional forgiveness doesn't always work to release you from the stress of a conflict," said Forgiveness.

"How so?" asked Revenge.

"Unconditional forgiveness allows your peace to immediately return to you, while contingent Forgiveness puts everything on hold until the conditions are met," said Forgiveness.

"Isn't that a little selfish?" asked Revenge.

"No," said Forgiveness.

"It sounds to me like you're more concerned about self-peace then you are about restoring a relationship," said Revenge.

"Don't get me wrong. Restoring a broken relationship is what forgiveness is really all about," said Forgiveness.

"Then unconditional forgiveness is not better than conditional forgiveness because conditional forgiveness has the potential for restoration," said Revenge.

"What you fail to understand is that there are basically two types of people we're talking about here. One type is searching for truth and the other type is not," said Forgiveness.

"Explain," said Revenge.

"Those that are not searching for truth cannot be restored by conditional forgiveness. So, unconditional forgiveness allows you to keep your peace while separating yourself from the situation. However, those that are searching for the truth have a higher potential for restoration when differences occur. Hence, conditional forgiveness would bring the two parties together to resolve the issue and forgiveness can be either sought or granted, thus restoring a relationship. The most important thing to remember is that you must learn how to discern the spirits of people who offend you so that you can use forgiveness effectively. If you do not, you will not know how or who it is that can be restored," said Forgiveness.

"That being the case, the Christian God is a God who offers only conditional forgiveness. Does He not?" asked Revenge.

"Yes." His forgiveness is conditional," said Forgiveness.

"Why? Most don't seek the truth," asked Revenge.

"Forgiveness is for those who do seek the truth," said Forgiveness.

"And what about all the others?" asked Revenge.

"They are not forgiven," said Forgiveness.

"Why?" asked Revenge.

"Because they will not forgive others," said Forgiveness.

"And what happens to them?" asked Revenge.

"They are separated from God," said Forgiveness.

"How can you tell who these people are?" asked Revenge.

"They are the people who pay back evil for evil," answered Forgiveness.

Life and Death Converse

"Is life a one-time event?" asked Death.

"No," said Life.

"How so?" asked Death.

"The worm never dies," said Life.

"What's that supposed to mean?" asked Death.

"It means that once a thing exists, it never dies," said Life.

"I don't believe that," said Death.

"Why not?" asked Life.

"For one, I've never seen anyone ever come back from the dead," said Death.

"Just because you don't see it in your lifetime doesn't mean that death is final," said Life.

"Give me credit for knowing something about death, for it is 'Death' that you're talking to," said Death.

"There's no denying that things die, but things rise again," said Life.

"Poppycock," said Death.

"Why do you say that?" asked Life.

"I have not seen a resurrection, and I have been around a long time," said Death.

"That's because the fullness of time has not arrived yet," said Life.

"What does the fullness of time mean?" asked Death.

"It means that life will defeat death by swallowing it up," said Life.

"Death will always be with us," said Death.

"It will not," said Life.

"That's not true and you know it," said Death.

"I know nothing of the sort," said Life.

"There can be no life without death nearby," said Death.

"You will be done away with some day," said Life.

"And what day will that be?" asked Death.

"On the day the new creation begins," said Life.

"I don't buy that at all," said Death.

"It will come to pass whether you buy it or not," said Life.

"Has not nature taught us that a tree can't live forever?" asked Death.

"Yes, but this nature that you're talking about is a fallen nature," said Life.

"What's that supposed to mean?" asked Death.

"It means creation was perverted because sin entered the world. Death was never God's intention," said Life.

"When did this sin pervert creation?" asked Death.

"Not long after it started," said Life.

"Who perverted it?" asked Death.

"Lucifer," said Life.

"Who is Lucifer?" asked Death.

"He was the Morning Star," said Life.

"Lucifer was a star?" asked Death.

"No, he was an angel," said Life.

"Where did he come from?" asked Death.

"He was created by God," said Life.

"Am I to understand that God is responsible for death entering the world?" asked Death.

"No, God is not responsible," said Life.

"Then who is?" asked Death.

"Pride is," said Life.

"How so?" asked Death.

"Lucifer wanted to be like 'the Most High God'", said Life.

"What else did he do?" asked Death.

"He left his designated place that was assigned to him and brought a third of the angles with him," said Life.

"What has all this got to do with death?" asked Death.

"Lucifer was in charge of God's creation. Hence, perversion entered the world," said Life.

"Am I to understand that this perversion you're talking about is death?" asked Death.

"God is Life. Hence, death cannot be found in Him or His creation," said Life.

"So I am a perversion of God's creation?" asked Death.

"Yes," said Life.

"If that's true, where was a person to be found before they were born? Also, why did God allow him to be born into a perverted creation?" asked Death.

"When a seed is perverted, its offspring is too," said Life.

"What does that mean?" asked Death.

"It means that when Adam and Eve fell their seed was perverted," said Life.

"Is that when sin came upon the earth?" asked Death.

"Yes," said Life.

"Was earth the last to be perverted?' asked Death.

"Yes, but there's a place being prepared where you will not reside," said Life.

"So death will be swallowed up and life will live on?" asked Death.

"Yes," said Life.

"Okay, none of what you say can be proven, but I can prove that death exists. Hence, death is an integral part of the natural order of things. You make it sound as if death is a bad thing, but I say that it's a good thing because it's the only way that things can keep on keeping on. A thing must die to make room for the next thing to live. It passes on its seed of life. Not a seed of death as you suggest," said Death.

"How can you call a seed that eventually dies a seed of life?" asked Life.

"Because it brings life, does it not?" asked Death.

"It brings life, but not eternal life," said Life.

"Why does life have to be eternal?" asked Death.

If it were not, all life would end eventually," said Life.

"Eternal Life is a man-made concept that has nothing to do with reality," said Death.

"The desire for life to be eternal is proof that fulfillment for that desire must exist. Just like the desire for a drink of water is proof that water exists," said Life.

"Can't you see that life and death are one?" asked Death.

"You can because of who you are. I cannot because of who I am," said Life.

"Was not a lion created to kill so that it could live?" asked Death.

"It was never God's intention; but the lion shall lay down by the lamb one day," said Life.

"That's ridiculous, the lion will devour the lamb because it has to eat," said Death.

"It will eat, but it will not eat the lamb," said Life.

"What will it eat?" asked Death.

"It will eat from a tree that gives life," said Life.

"Will it eat fruit from the tree?" asked Death.

"It will not have to eat," said Life.

"When a man dies, is he aware of self?" asked Death.

"No," said Life.

"What! Then he's dead," said Death.

"No! He sleeps until judgment day," said Life.

"No man is conscious when he dies?" asked Death.

"None," said Life.

"Why?" asked Death.

"So that those that are dead would not have an advantage over those that are living," said Life.

"And what advantage would that be?" asked Death.

"The advantage of experiencing God," said Life.

"Are you saying that it is better to be with God than it is to live here on earth?" asked Death.

"Both are good, but it is better to be with God," said Life.

"There is no God. Hence, death is final," said Death.

"You are the deliverer of death. Hence, you can see no other way," said Life.

"Everything dies, just look around you," said Death.

"Not true," said Life.

"Show me this Lucifer and I will believe that it is possible that things can exist without dying," said Death.

"Hast thou not seen his handy-work?" asked Life.

"I don't know what you mean," said Death.

"If you have seen death, you have seen Lucifer. Lucifer and death are one," said Life.

"Okay, show me life," said Death.

"Life cannot be shown to death," said Life.

"Why not?" asked Death.

"There is no life in death, just like there is no light in darkness," said Life.

"I see life and death every day," said Death.

"The life that you see is really dead," said Life.

"What do you mean?" asked Death.

"I mean there are two kinds of life," said Life.

"Explain," said Death.

"There is a physical life and a spiritual life. The one that you see is the physical life that is dead to the spiritual life," said Life.

"Are you saying that it's possible to be dead at the same time you're alive?" asked Death.

"Absolutely," said Life.

"Are there people around who are alive physically and spiritually?" asked Death.

"Yes, but not many," said Life.

"Where are they to be found?" asked Death.

"Why do you ask? Do you desire to visit death upon them?" asked Life.

"You said that Lucifer and death are one, did you not?" asked Death.

"I have a question for you," said Life.

"What is it?" asked Death.

"Why do you ask so many questions?" asked Life.

"To show that death has power over life," said Death.

"Although it is within thy power to visit death upon my creation, it is for but a short time. Know this for a fact: life will swallow you up," said Life.

"Death shows no signs of being swallowed up by you," said Death.

"It has already happened," said Life.

"Why would anyone want to live forever?" asked Death.

"To experience all that God has to offer," said Life.

"I can't imagine anything more beautiful than what we have already seen. And seventy years, plus or minus, is enough time to see it," said Death.

"It has not entered the mind of man the things that God has prepared for His people," said Life.

"In my opinion, death is a hedge against boredom and that's why it's necessary," said Death.

"That's because you have tunnel vision and think of only one thing," said Life.

"And what might that one thing be?" asked Death.

"That which is dead can only think of dead things and that which is alive can only think of living things," said Life.

"No matter what you say, the fact is, death is all around us and it will continue to remain that way forever," said Death.

"That's because you see only the physical world and not the spiritual world," said Life.

"Show me the spiritual world," said Death.

"You have already seen it," said Life.

"When?" asked Death.

"Upon awakening," said Life.

"Upon awakening?" asked Death.

"Yes, upon awakening you leave the spiritual world and re-enter the physical world and, for a brief moment, you're aware of both worlds simultaneously, but you must leave one to stay in the other," said Life.

"Are you talking about sleep?" asked Death.

"Yes," said Life.

"Are you proposing that when we're asleep, we enter the spiritual world?" asked Death.

"Yes, and you have no control over that world," said Life.

"What do you mean?" asked Death.

"I mean the spirits in your dream cannot be held at bay like they can when you're awake," said Life.

"I don't understand," said Death.

"The dream world is the mind minus gravity's influence on the body," said Life.

"What has that got to do with life and death?" asked Death.

"It is gravity's effect on the body that deadens one's sensitivity to spiritual things. When one sleeps, this effect is minimized. Hence in sleep we become more aware of the spiritual world as it relates to life and death," said Life.

"What do you mean by 'As it relates to life and death'?" asked Death.

"Issues of life and death are played out in a man's sleep," said Life.

"I'm not getting it," said Death.

"Dreams show the differential between the real life and the pretentious death," said life.

"So...?" said Death.

"Dreams are showing you that death has entered you. Hence all is not well," said Life.

"So...?" said Death.

"What would be the purpose of showing this if in the end, all things die?" asked Life.

"There is no purpose other than the purpose of satisfying the five senses," said Death.

"For now, my purpose is to defeat death," said Life.

"Without death, life is not possible," said Death.

"Death's effect on life has only caused it to be intermittent for a short time; but, when things are restored, life will once again be continuous," said Life.

"I will always exist as long as there are living things," said Death.

"There are things living now that know not Death," said Life.

"And what might those things be?" asked Death.

"The angels who have not followed Lucifer," said Life.

"Where are they now?" asked Death.

"They are in principalities in high places," said Life.

"What are they doing?" asked Death.

"They war against you," said Life.

"I have not seen them," said Death.

"They work in secret," said Life.

"It doesn't look like they're doing very well," said Death.

"That's because they're restricted," said Life.

"How so?" asked Death.

"They must be prayed down to do their work," said Life.

"Prayed down? What do you mean?" asked Death.

"Man must ask for help to come," said Life.

"Today's man would never believe that," said Death.

"You're right. It is written that, in the last days, man will perish for a lack of knowledge," said Life.

"And what knowledge will he be lacking?" asked Death.

"That there is life after death," said Life.

Free Speech and Restraint Converse

"Is not freedom of speech the best thing that ever happened to mankind?" asked Free Speech.

"It's a two-edge sword that will eventually dishearten all who listen to her voice on a regular basis," said Restraint.

"The pluses definitely outweigh the negatives," said Free Speech.

"In the long run everyone is damaged by too much freedom of speech," said Restraint.

"And what damage is that?" asked Free Speech.

"The decline of morals and the growth of cynicism," said Restraint.

"It is worth the price to keep the information flowing," said Free Speech.

"Its way too much information," said Restraint.

"No one is forced to listen. They can always turn it off," said Free Speech.

"They never do and you bank on it," said Restraint.

"You can't blame that on me," said Free Speech.

"Yes, I can," said Restraint.

"How so?" asked Free Speech.

"You entice," said Restraint.

"What's wrong with that?" asked Free Speech.

"It leads to embellishing," said Restraint.

"What's so bad about that?" asked Free Speech.

"It's deception, and that's evil," said Restraint.

"So what should we do, censor everything because of a little deception?" asked Free Speech.

"We should release information based on the wisdom of releasing it. Not on the basis of commercial benefits," said Restraint.

"Advertisers have figured out what people want and they give it to them. What's wrong with that?" asked Free Speech.

"Advertisers don't care about what's good for society. They only care about money," said Restraint.

"There's no way to control that," said Free Speech.

"You're right; you're out of control," said Restraint.

"People have to buy and sell," said Free Speech.

"Not murder, rape, and rob, just to mention a few," said Restraint.

"I don't understand," said Free Speech.

"There should never be a movie or a book written about murder just to entertain someone," said Restraint.

"What would you do about profanity, pornography?" asked Free Speech.

"There would be none of that," said Restraint.

"Why?" asked Free Speech.

"There's no sane reason to protect the right to express such base things," said Restraint.

"What about the right to call someone a jerk?" asked Free Speech.

"You can do it, but do it at your own risk," said Restraint.

"What does that mean?" asked Free Speech.

"It means that there would be no law that would protect you when you call your neighbor a jerk, and no time in jail if your neighbor punches you," said Restraint.

"And who is my neighbor?" asked Free Speech.

"Everyone," said Restraint.

"What about political debates?" asked Free Speech.

"What about them?" asked Restraint.

"Well, is it okay to misrepresent your opponent for political gain?" asked Free Speech.

"Do you realize how ridiculous that sounds?" asked Restraint.

"Everyone does it. It's the norm," said Free Speech.

"It is written that in the last days they will call good bad, and bad good," said Restraint.

"How are you going to get people to use restraint? You're not! That's why you have to extend free speech with no limits and hope it'll be used wisely," said Free Speech.

"Free speech in the mouths of scoundrels cheapens it," said Restraint.

"Who might these scoundrels be?" asked Free Speech.

"All those who would use it unwisely," said Restraint.

"Who is wise?" asked Free Speech.

"Not many," said Restraint.

"Are you advocating limiting free speech?" asked Free Speech.

"Not to the average citizen, but to those who hold power," said Restraint.

"Why?" asked Free Speech.

"If the leaders restrain their free speech, their followers will, too," said Restraint.

"So you want the leaders to show an example of how free speech should be exercised?" asked Free Speech.

"This should also apply to all public figures," said Restraint.

"Give me an example," said Free Speech.

"Anyone who appears on television, radio, newspapers," said Restraint.

"That's never going to happen," said Free Speech.
"It will when the whole thing collapses," said Restraint.

"That'll never happen. It's got a life of its own," said Free Speech.

"Free speech will eventually lead to most freedoms being taken away," said Restraint.

"Why do you say that?" asked Free Speech.

"It will eventually expose too much, becoming a threat to those who hold power," said Restraint.

"How can we safeguard against this happening?" asked Free Speech.

"By self-restraint," said Restraint.

"Not going to happen," said Free Speech.

"I know," said Restraint.

"People will always choose freedom over restraint," said Free Speech.

"That's because it sounds good on the surface; but, what they don't realize is that no one has ever seen freedom run it's full circle in modern times," said Restraint.

"Where might we be in the circle?" asked Free Speech.

"About 300 out of 360 degrees!" said Restraint.

"Where do you get that figure from?" asked Free Speech.

"From prophesy," said Restraint.

"What prophesy?" asked Free Speech.

"The one that says love will grow cold and children will turn against their parents and the young will teach the old," said Restraint.

"I don't see love growing cold. I see a lot of love and good in the world," said Free Speech.

"Look closer," said Restraint.

"You see what you want to see," said Free Speech.

CELESTIAL DIALOGUES

"When you're not caught up into the things of this world, you see things clearer," said Restraint.

"Extending freedom is the best that man can do," said Free Speech.

"This is a true statement," said Restraint.

"If this is true then how can God condemn us for exercising a full measure of free speech?" asked Free Speech.

"You're-exercising a full measure of free will, not Free speech," said Restraint.

"Well then, you agree with me that freedom is a good thing?" asked Free Speech.

"Freedom, plus the Ten Commandments, is a good thing," said Restraint.

"Of course," said Free Speech.

"The Ten Commandments are not being adhered to," said Restraint.

"People make mistakes," said Free Speech.

"People ignore the commandments for personal gain," said Restraint.

"People ignore them because they have not the fear of God in them," said Free Speech.

"Ah! We have traveled the full circle," said Restraint.

"What do you mean?" asked Free Speech.

"You just said it. The root of freedom is really freedom from God's laws," said Restraint.

"Are you suggesting that the pursuit of absolute freedom is really man replacing God's laws with his own laws?" asked Free Speech.

"Yes, I am," said Restraint.

"The Founding Fathers of freedom were God fearing," said Free Speech.

"True, but that was the Founding Fathers. Freedom has come to mean something entirely different because the people are different today," said Restraint.

"Things change," said Free Speech.

"They have indeed," said Restraint.

"We have the law; there is no need for a God in the Constitution," said Free Speech.

"The law is weak because man is inconsistent," said Restraint.

"So?" asked Free Speech.

"The more freedom you extend, the more the laws are unenforceable," said Restraint.

"Anything is better than repression," said Free Speech.

"True, repression is bad, but there's a fine balance here," said Restraint.

"Balance is hard to obtain when you grant total freedom," said Free Speech.

"There's only one thing that'll give balance to freedom," said Restraint.

"What might that be?" asked Free Speech.

"Fear," said Restraint.

CELESTIAL DIALOGUES

"But with fear you can't really have total freedom," said Free Speech.

"Thank you! I rest my case," said Restraint.

Spirituality and Religion Converse

"Will your religion save you?" asked Spirituality.

"I hope," said Religion.

"So your religion is based on hope?" asked Spirituality.

"Yes, hope bridges the gap between despair and unbelief," said Religion.

"Explain," asked Spirituality.

"When something is desired, but it is in the distant future, it is hope that gets you there," said Religion.

"How is that different from faith?" asked Spirituality.

"I think they are one and the same," said Religion.

"It seems to me that hope is weaker than faith," said Spirituality.

"How so?" asked Religion.

"It seems to me that, if you have faith, you can become convinced of something, whereas if you have only hope, you can still be in doubt," said Spirituality.

"My religion says that we look for the hope that is within us to come," said Religion.

"Is that why you go to church?" asked Spirituality.

"I go to church because that's what my religion teaches me I should do," said Religion.

"Do you regard yourself as a religious person?" asked Spirituality.

"Yes," said Religion.

"Why?" asked Spirituality.

"Because I practice my religion," said Religion.

"So by following certain religious practices, you think that makes you acceptable to God?" asked Spirituality.

"Yes, it's an outward sign for all to see that I believe in God," said Religion.

"What about an inward sign?" asked Spirituality.

"I'm not sure I know what you mean," said Religion.

"Is there something in you that actually knows God?" asked Spirituality.

"What do you mean by something in me?" asked Religion.

"Is God's Spirit actually in you?" asked Spirituality.

"I don't know and I don't think it matters as long as I go to church and worship God," said Religion.

"It is written that God's people will worship Him in truth and in spirit. Did you not know that?" asked Spirituality.

"I worship God by keeping His ordinances," said Religion.

"Which do you feel is more important, keeping God's ordinances or worshiping God in spirit?" asked Spirituality.

"What do you mean by worshiping in spirit?" asked Religion.

"I mean that which is flesh is flesh and that which is spirit is spirit," said Spirituality.

"Are you suggesting that my religion is of the flesh and, therefore, not acceptable to God?" asked Religion.

"I'm suggesting that you can't know God through the practice of religion, while at the same time ignoring God's Spirit," said Spirituality.

"I try to keep God's commandments," said Religion.

"Do you not know that it is impossible to keep God's commandments?" asked Spirituality.

"I do the best that I can do," said Religion.

"Your best is not good enough," said Spirituality.

"I know that, and that's why I believe Jesus died for me and paid for all my shortcomings," said Religion.

"If that's true, then why are you still trying to please God with your religious practices?" asked Spirituality.

"Because that's what our pastor teaches we should do," said Religion.

"Did he ever teach you that there will be many false teachers who will lead many astray? Did he ever teach you that there will be those who think that they know God, but that God won't know them even though they go to church and study their Bibles?" asked Spirituality.

"I'm sure that doesn't apply to me," said Religion.

"Be assured, your religion has nothing to do with spirituality," said Spirituality.

"Okay, what is spirituality?" asked Religion.

"First of all, religion is not spirituality. Spirituality has more to do with the essence or the soul of a particular thing, but not the thing itself," said Spirituality.

"Give me an example," said Religion.

"A smile shows joy within a person, but the smile itself is not joy," said Spirituality.

"So!" said Religion.

"You can have religion and still not have joy," said Spirituality.

"So!" said Religion.

"Do you not remember what I said about worshiping God in truth and in spirit?" asked Spirituality.

"Yes, but so what?" asked Religion.

"God knows those who get the essence of His Spirit and those who do not," said Spirituality.

"Are you talking about the essence of God or God's actual Spirit?" asked Religion.

"Take your pick," said Spirituality.

"I don't know if I want to believe that," said Religion.

"Why?" asked Spirituality.

"It is so much easier to follow a rule than it is to follow the spirit behind the rule," said Religion.

"That's because it requires spiritual discernment, whereas religion does not," said Spirituality.

"It does seem that way," said Religion.

"True religion is experienced in the soul and does not reside in the mind or in the body," said Spirituality.

"Give me an example," said Religion.

"It's possible to be sitting in church while at the same time God is the furthest thing from your mind. This would not be worshiping God in spirit but rather worshiping Him with your mind and body only," said Spirituality.

"Is that what Jesus meant when He said, 'My people know me and I know them'?" asked Religion.

"Exactly," said Spirituality.

"Are religious people deceiving themselves?" asked Religion.

"They're not deceiving themselves. They have fallen asleep spiritually," said Spirituality.

"What do you mean by that?" asked Religion.

"Religion gives them a false sense of security and lures them into a spiritual coma, whereas spirituality demands that you always be in the now moment. Which is the only place where the Spirit of God can be found," said Spirituality.

"This is scary. At the same time, it is exciting," said Religion.

"It's exciting because that's where true life resides. It is scary because that is where death resides," said Spirituality.

"So walking in the spirit is life, and walking in the flesh leads to death?" asked Religion.

"Yes, that is what is meant by 'the Spirit is life'," said Spirituality.

"Does that mean that it's not necessary to go to church?" asked Religion.

"What do you mean by church?" asked Spirituality.

"You know, your local church," said Religion.

"A church is not a building," said Spirituality.

"What is it?" asked Religion.

"The church is the believers, not the building," said Spirituality.

"But I love the building. That's the church to me," said Religion.

"So did the Sadducees and the Pharisees," said Spirituality.

"What do you mean by that?" asked Religion.

"The Sadducees and Pharisees prided themselves on keeping the Sabbath, but did not recognize Jesus Christ (called the Lord of the Sabbath) when He showed up," said Spirituality.

"Are you saying that pride in one's religion can actually be a detriment to one's spirituality?" asked Religion.

"Absolutely," said Spirituality.

"Do you mean that a person can spend his whole life doing religious things and still end up not knowing anything about spirituality?" asked Religion.

"Yes, I'm afraid that is true," said Spirituality.

"There are millions of people that don't realize this," said Religion.

"This is true. They have a form of godliness, but they deny the power there of," said Spirituality.

"What does that mean?" asked Religion.

"It means that they believe in God, but deny the power of spiritual things in their lives," said Spirituality.

"Does this mean they have a false sense of security?" asked Religion.

"According to Christian doctrine, they do," said Spirituality.

"What should these Christians do?" asked Religion.

"They should stop with their religious practices and seek spiritual enlightenment," said Spirituality.

"Where can they find this spiritual enlightenment?" asked Religion.

"It is found within the man," said Spirituality.

"What exactly does that mean?" asked Religion.

"It means that the kingdom of God is within a man; hence, it cannot be found in a building," said Spirituality.

"How does one go inside one's self to find spirituality?" asked Religion.

"By seeking it," said Spirituality.

"But how do I seek it?" asked Religion.

"You have already sought it," said Spirituality.

"How so?" asked Religion.

"When you ask questions, it means that you're seeking," said Spirituality.

"Then why don't I have it?" asked Religion.

"Because the faith that you need to find it comes from another source," said Spirituality.

"Where does it come from?" asked Religion.

"It comes from God," said Spirituality.

"What has that got to do with anything?" asked Religion.

"Only God's Spirit—and not religion—can cause your dead spirit to come alive again," said Spirituality.

"What do you mean 'come alive again'?" asked Religion.

"I mean that people are fallen, until their spirits are quickened by God's Spirit," said Spirituality.

"I still don't understand," said Religion.

"When a man is first born, he's born spiritually dead. It isn't until the second birth that his spirit is reborn," said Spirituality.

"And how might the second birth take place?" asked Religion.

"One is drawn by God's Spirit," said Spirituality.

"How does that work?" asked Religion.

"God draws you by circumstances in your life, sometimes over a long period of time and sometimes instantly," said Spirituality.

"God's Spirit hasn't drawn me as of yet," said Religion.

"That's because, up until now, you have not desired it, mainly because you've preferred religion over spiritual things," said Spirituality.

"What makes you think that I desire it now?" asked Religion.

"By the many questions you ask," said Spirituality.

"I'm just curious," said Religion.

"You are more than curious," said Spirituality.

"You take away my religion, you take away everything I believe in," said Religion.

"There's no denying that there's much comfort in religion. That's why the churches are full of dead people," said Spirituality.

"What will happen to me when God's Spirit enters me?" asked Religion.

"It will complete your religion by rejuvenating your spirit," said Spirituality.

"What do you mean?" asked Religion.

"It will put your religion in its proper place," said Spirituality.

"So there is a place for religion?" asked Religion.

"Absolutely," said Spirituality.

"And where might that place be?" asked Religion.

"Wherever the Spirit leads on that particular day," said Spirituality.

For those who believe in prayer

Wonder not why your prayers
have a built-in delay,
if granting a request
takes you more than a day.

Spiritual Discernment

When I meet you
you don't meet me.
When you meet me
you meet you.

My Aphorisms

- If you truly forgive, your enemies they should be able to make a request of you.
- Beauty is designed to trap.
- Seeing recognizable images robs the imagination.
- In order for the past to exist, it must take up residency in the now.
- Keep quiet if you don't want to reveal your spirit.
- To live in a world of pretense is to never know where you really stand.
- Freedom plus the Ten Commandments is better than democracy by itself.
- Freedom of speech will eventually lead to most freedoms being taken away.
- The soul cannot reconcile both good and evil -- you must choose one.
- The difference between a miracle and a prayer is speed.
- Soap and forgiveness serves the same purpose.
- Realize that when you pay taxes you're being treated as foreigners in your own country.
- Forgiveness will cut your enemies list by one hundred percent.
- When you judge others, God lets them off the hook.
- Mountains won't move if you won't move when someone makes a request of you.

About the Author

Frank Stapleton was born and raised in Baltimore. Frank lives with his wife, Mary, in Northern Baltimore County and has two adult daughters. Frank likes to create abstracts paintings because he believes it engages the imagination. He's also an inventor with a background in Human Factors Engineering. One of his inventions was successful enough to allow him to follow his passion for writing even though he has no formal training. He likes to think of himself as a spiritual contemplator.

www.ingramcontent.com/pod-product-compliance
Lightning Source LLC
LaVergne TN
LVHW041255080426
835510LV00009B/748